WRITERS AND THEIR WORK

ISOBEL ARMSTRONG
*Consultant Editor*

# PRE-ROMANTIC POETRY

# PRE-ROMANTIC POETRY

## Vincent Quinn

© Copyright 2012 by Vincent Quinn

First published in 2012 by Northcote House Publishers Ltd, Horndon House, Horndon, Tavistock, Devon, PL19 9NQ, United Kingdom. Tel: +44 (0) 1822 810066  Fax: +44 (0) 1822 810034.

**British Library Cataloguing-in-Publication Data**
A catalogue record for this book is available from the British Library

ISBN 978-0-7463-1183-7 hardcover
ISBN 978-0-7463-1188-2 paperback

Typeset by PDQ Typesetting, Newcastle-under-Lyme
Printed and bound in the United Kingdom

For my Family

# Contents

# Acknowledgements

I owe many thanks to Clare Brant, for first conveying the excitement of eighteenth-century writing to me, and to Susan Manning, for confirming that excitement. This book probably wouldn't exist without their guidance and scholarly example. I am also very grateful to Isobel Armstrong for commissioning the study, and to the anonymous reader who commented so positively on it.

Current and former colleagues in the Department of English, Drama and Comparative Literature at the University of Sussex have provided a rewarding atmosphere in which to work. In particular I want to acknowledge information, advice and support from Alistair Davies, Amber Jacobs, Laura Marcus, Denise de Caires Narain, Stephanie Newell, Nicholas Royle, Jenny Bourne Taylor and Norman Vance.

For friendship and inspiration, I would also like to thank Helen Barr, Louise Hudd, the late and greatly missed Siobhán Kilfeather, David Marriott, Andy Medhurst, Noam Raz, Yael Raz, Lindsay Smith, and Sophie Thomas. I am especially grateful to Vicky Lebeau and Alan Sinfield who were kind enough to read the book in draft form: their attentive responses, and their belief in the project, have been invaluable.

Finally – but most importantly – I want to acknowledge the unique contributions of my father Sean Quinn, my late mother Lena Quinn, my brothers, and my sister. They have my love and gratitude, and this book is for them.

# Biographical Outlines

| | |
|---|---|
| 1688 | Alexander Pope born. |
| 1700 | James Thomson born. |
| 1709 | Alexander Pope, *Pastorals*. |
| 1713 | Alexander Pope, *Windsor Forest*. |
| 1716 | Thomas Gray born. |
| 1720 | Elizabeth Montagu born (*née* Robinson). |
| 1721 | William Collins born. |
| 1722 | Mary Leapor born. |
| | Christopher Smart born. |
| 1725 | Thomas Gray becomes friends with Richard West and Horace Walpole at Eton. |
| 1730 | Oliver Goldsmith born. |
| | James Thomson, *The Seasons*. |
| 1731 | William Cowper born. |
| 1735 | James Thomson, first three parts of *Liberty*. |
| 1736 | James Thomson, last two parts of *Liberty*. |
| | James Macpherson born. |
| 1739 | Thomas Gray on Grand Tour with Horace Walpole. |
| 1741 | Thomas Gray quarrels with Horace Walpole and returns to England alone. |
| 1742 | Richard West dies. |
| | Thomas Gray moves to Cambridge, where he is based for the rest of his life. |
| | William Collins, *Persian Eclogues*. |
| 1744 | Alexander Pope dies. |
| 1745 | Hannah More born. |
| | Thomas Gray and Horace Walpole resume contact. |
| 1746 | Mary Leapor dies. |
| | William Collins, *Odes on Several Descriptive and Allegoric Subjects*. |

| | |
|---|---|
| 1748 | James Thomson dies shortly after publishing *The Castle of Indolence*.<br>William Collins, 'Ode Occasioned by the Death of Mr Thomson'.<br>Mary Leapor, *Poems Upon Several Occasions*. |
| 1752 | Thomas Chatterton born.<br>Ann Yearsley (*née* Cromartie) born.<br>Christopher Smart, *Poems on Several Occasions*. |
| 1753 | Thomas Gray, *Six Poems with Designs by Mr Bentley*. |
| 1754 | George Crabbe born. |
| 1757 | William Blake born.<br>Thomas Gray, *Odes*; Gray declines the Poet Laureateship. |
| 1759 | Robert Burns born.<br>William Collins dies. |
| 1760 | James Macpherson, *Fragments of Ancient Poetry, Collected in the Highlands of Scotland*. |
| 1762 | James Macpherson, *Fingal, an Ancient Epic Poem*. |
| 1763 | James Macpherson, *Temora*.<br>William Cowper attempts suicide for the first time and is placed in Dr Nathaniel Cotton's asylum in St Albans. |
| 1764 | William Cowper converts to Evangelical Christianity.<br>Oliver Goldsmith, *The Traveller, or A Prospect of Society*. |
| 1765 | William Cowper leaves Dr Cotton's asylum; five months later he takes up residence with the Unwin family in Huntingdon. |
| 1767 | William Cowper meets John Newton; following the death of Mrs Unwin's husband, Cowper moves with Mary Unwin to Newton's parish in Olney, Buckinghamshire. |
| 1768 | Thomas Gray, *Poems by Mr Gray*. |
| 1769 | Elizabeth Montagu, *Essay on the Writings and Genius of Shakespeare*. |
| 1770 | Thomas Chatterton commits suicide.<br>William Wordsworth born.<br>Priscilla Pointon, *Poems on Several Occasions*.<br>Oliver Goldsmith, *The Deserted Village*. |
| 1771 | Thomas Gray dies.<br>Christopher Smart dies. |
| 1772 | S. T. Coleridge born. |

| | |
|---|---|
| 1773 | William Cowper becomes convinced he is damned and enters into a severe depression; another suicide attempt. |
| 1774 | Oliver Goldsmith dies. |
| 1777 | Thomas Chatterton, *Poems*. |
| 1779 | William Cowper and John Newton, *Olney Hymns*. |
| 1781 | William Cowper meets Lady Austen; they clash towards the end of the year. |
| 1782 | William Cowper, *Poems by William Cowper, of the Inner Temple, Esq.*; Cowper and Lady Austen reconciled. |
| 1783 | George Crabbe, *The Village*. |
| 1784 | William Cowper and Lady Austen quarrel irrevocably. |
| 1785 | William Cowper, *The Task*; Cowper begins translating Homer and resumes contact with his cousin, Lady Hesketh. |
| | Ann Yearsley, *Poems on Several Occasions*; Yearsley breaks with Hannah More. |
| 1786 | William Cowper and Mary Unwin move to Weston Underwood. |
| | Robert Burns, *Poems, chiefly in the Scottish Dialect*. |
| 1787 | William Cowper's third serious depression. |
| | Ann Yearsley, *Poems on Various Subjects*. |
| 1791 | William Cowper finishes translating Homer; strokes leave Mary Unwin incapacitated until her death in 1796. |
| 1794 | William Cowper suffers a fourth major depression and stops writing poetry; this bout lasts until his death. |
| 1795 | John Keats born. |
| 1796 | Robert Burns dies. |
| | James Macpherson dies. |
| | Ann Yearsley, *The Rural Lyre*. |
| 1798 | S. T. Coleridge and William Wordsworth, first edition of the *Lyrical Ballads*. |
| 1800 | William Cowper dies. |
| | Elizabeth Montagu dies. |
| | William Wordsworth, 'Preface' to the second edition of the *Lyrical Ballads*. |
| 1806 | Ann Yearsley dies. |

# Abbreviations and References

CTG     *Correspondence of Thomas Gray*, edited by Paget Toynbee and Leonard Whibley, with Corrections and Additions by H.W. Starr, 3 vols (Oxford: Clarendon Press, 1971)

EWP     *Eighteenth-Century Women Poets: An Oxford Anthology*, edited by Roger Lonsdale (Oxford and New York: Oxford University Press, 1989)

GCG     *The Poems of Thomas Gray, William Collins and Oliver Goldsmith*, edited by Roger Lonsdale (London and New York: Longman, 1969)

LWC     *The Letters and Prose Writings of William Cowper*, edited by James King and Charles Ryskamp, 5 vols (Oxford: Clarendon Press, 1979–1986)

PAP     *The Poems of Alexander Pope: A One-Volume Edition of the Twickenham Text with Selected Annotations*, edited by John Butt (Bungay: Methuen, 1963)

PWC     *The Poems of William Cowper*, edited by John H. Baird and Charles Ryskamp, 3 vols (Oxford: Clarendon Press, 1980–1995)

# Note on the Text

When possible, I have used the standard editions of the letters and poems of the writers I discuss – this has involved preserving some unorthodox spellings, especially in the letters of Thomas Gray. Where there is no modern collected edition available, I have quoted from readily-available anthologies rather than from eighteenth-century sources.

# 1

## Pre-Romanticism and Literary History

In a letter written in the late 1730s, the poet Thomas Gray gives a 'true & faithful Narrative' of how his 'very tranquil' studies are 'suddenly alarmd with a great hubbub of Tongues'. The voices do not come from the street as one might think. Instead they are produced by his books. Madame de Sévigné, the seventeenth-century letter writer, complains that Aristotle is squeezing her sixth volume to death but Aristotle insists that he has 'as much right to be here as you'. De Sévigné's cousin, the Comte de Bussy, refuses to help because he himself is being killed by Strabo, the ancient geographer. Finding himself beside Euclid, Nicholas Boileau wonders why 'any Man of Sense will have a Mathematician in his Study'. Agreeing, Jonathan Swift suggests that 'Metaphysicians and Natural Philosophers' should be the next to go. Meanwhile John Locke speculates that 'our owner must have very confused ideas, to jumble us so strangely together' (*CTG* i 93–4).

As well as revealing the heterogeneous knowledge that would later inform Gray's poetry, the letter prompts questions about the relationship between culture and history. Like all books, this current study emerges from its own 'hubbub of Tongues'. And like all writers I have had to hush some voices while amplifying others. The literary-historical conventions that I have inherited, however, do not allow me to arrange those voices with complete freedom. If I were to place Swift before Strabo, or Euclid after Locke, I would have to justify my apparent disregard of historical sequence. The second half of this introduction will use Thomas Gray's letter to argue that such linearity can be both limiting and misleading. But before presenting my case for a non-sequential version of literary history, I want to explore the meaning and repercussions of the term 'pre-romantic'. As well as presenting an alternative approach to the poetry of the mid- and late-eighteenth-century, this section will argue that the invention of 'pre-romanticism' is typical of the processes by which literary criticism diminishes certain forms of writing in order to privilege others. In other words, pre-romanticism is a constructed category, and its construction illuminates the larger workings of literary history.

## DEFINING PRE-ROMANTICISM

Three decades ago the story of mid- to late-eighteenth-century poetry would have been restricted to a handful of much anthologized but little read poets (all of them male): James Thomson, William Collins, Oliver Goldsmith, William Cowper, Thomas Chatterton, Christopher Smart and Thomas Gray. In being yoked together, these writers would have been presented as preparing the ground for William Wordsworth and S. T. Coleridge. That is, they would have been 'pre-romantic'. This comfortable literary-historical narrative resembles the tranquillity that reigns in Gray's study before the anarchic events described in his letter. However just as the eighteenth-century poet's expectations are upset by his talkative books, so too have received versions of eighteenth-century poetry been disturbed, for the better, by three revolutionary anthologies.

Although twenty years have passed since the first of them was published, it's hard to overstate the continuing importance of *The New Oxford Book of Eighteenth-Century Verse* (1984) and *Eighteenth-Century Women Poets: An Oxford Anthology* (1989), both edited by Roger Lonsdale, and *The New Oxford Book of Romantic Period Verse* (1993), edited by Jerome McGann. These – and the anthologies that they've inspired – have restored neglected writers, unearthed forgotten ones, revealed surprising conti-nuities, and questioned existing assumptions. In doing so the Lonsdale and McGann volumes suggest that, for all their usefulness as shorthand, literary-historical categories impose a misleading unity onto the complex bodies of writing that circulate at any given moment. In other words 'romantic period' writing is very different from 'romantic' writing.

Given that the title of this book includes the word 'pre-romantic' I evidently find some value in literary-historical concepts. However there is no denying that this particular label creates as many problems as it solves. To make an obvious comparison, the term 'Pre-Raphaelite' was explicitly adopted by Dante Gabriel Rossetti and his circle whereas 'pre-romantic' has been applied by critics retrospectively. Moreover the Pre-Raphaelite Brotherhood was a mid-nineteenth-century movement that celebrated the art of Raphael's fifteenth-century predecessors: therefore although its members were defying chronology by allying themselves with the past, they were choosing a version of the past that was known to them. But if Wordsworth, Byron and Coleridge did not know that literary history would label them 'romantic' how could the previous generation of English poets have known that they were 'pre-romantic'?

As is often the case with literary history, there is a circular relationship between the genre and its examples: pre-romanticism is said to include Gray, Cowper and Goldsmith. Meanwhile Gray, Cowper and Goldsmith are said to define pre-romanticism. But if pre-romanticism is not a self-conscious identity, what do critics mean by the term? Why these authors? Which characteristics have led to the grouping? Again problems arise through literary history's selectiveness. The poets listed above are said to show a quasi-romantic sensitivity to nature plus an interest in interiority and extreme emotions. Additionally, Gray and Collins had depressive breakdowns, Smart was hospitalized for mania, Chatterton killed himself, and Cowper attempted suicide on at least two occasions. They therefore fit the popular association between madness, inspiration and Romantic genius.

However this narrative suppresses awkward details. As well as his pastoral classic, *The Seasons* (1726–30), James Thomson wrote such tub-thumping propaganda as 'Rule, Britannia' (1740); indeed *The Seasons* is itself a jingoistic poem. He also belonged to an earlier generation than the writers with whom he is most often grouped. Contrastingly, Thomas Chatterton, William Blake and Robert Burns were born in the 1750s yet the latter two are usually classified as romantic while Chatterton is not. Presumably life span has something to do with it. If Chatterton hadn't taken poison at the age of seventeen he, too, could have graduated to full romantic status. George Crabbe, however, fits neither grouping even though he, like the other three, was born in the 1750s. His continuing neglect may be due to his satiric accounts of provincial life: pre-romanticism isn't supposed to be funny, even though it often is (as Chapters 2 and 3 will show). Meanwhile the writers who feature most prominently in accounts of pre-romanticism – Gray and Cowper – were born over fifteen years apart. This makes it hard to talk about a single pre-romantic generation.

Two things should already be clear. First, 'pre-romanticism' is an unstable designation and, second, its rank has always been lower than 'romanticism'. Literary history not only produces simplified categories, it also creates a ranking system in which some periods (such as the late-eighteenth century) are deemed transitional. Caught between the more culturally valued groupings of early-eighteenth-century 'neo-classicism' and early-nineteenth-century 'romanticism', the fate of pre-romantic poetry is to be both premature and immature. However such marginalizations are inevitable given literary history's drift towards teleology. That is, literary-historical concepts such as 'transition' imply a future that is already inevitable. In doing so, they re-write diversity and uneven development by imagining cultural change as an ongoing movement towards a knowable (and narratable) present. As a consequence, bodies of work are either belated, or preparatory, or both. It therefore becomes even more difficult to recover what mid-eighteenth-century writers thought they were doing: instead we read them backwards, through what follows.

Problematic though it is, the term has received a major boost from Marshall Brown's *Preromanticism* (1991). Brown's intervention deserves full consideration, both for its weight and for the authority it brings to its subject. (The book is three hundred pages long and was published by a major university press.) However Brown's approach is not without problems. Brown is right to criticize some commentators for inventing a self-contradictory 'romantisme avant la lettre' in which pre-romantic writers are, in effect, already writing the same types of poetry as Wordsworth and Coleridge. However I am less comfortable when he argues that although 'the term "preromanticism" has always been attacked for its teleology' the 'real

4

problem with earlier studies of preromanticism is that they are not teleological enough'. Instead Brown claims that late-eighteenth-century writing is characterized by a vocal crisis in which 'the greatest authors in their greatest moments engaged in rigorously controlled struggles towards new modes of expression'. Then, 'when new resources were found – and it happened with astonishing suddenness for Wordsworth... and for those who underwent the impact of the new philosophy – the floodgates opened'.[1] In other words, pre-romantic writers matter not on their own terms but because they made romanticism possible.

It is certainly true that some eighteenth-century writers were anxiously aware of what W. Jackson Bate has called 'the burden of the past' – the difficulty, that is, of following such influential and prolific writers as Edmund Spenser and John Milton.[2] However Brown's unquestioning insistence on literary value weakens his argument. By accepting as 'inescapable' the 'fact' that the late-eighteenth-century saw a 'crisis of expression' in which 'masterpieces are few, and no major author of the period produced with anything like the ease of a Pope or a Wordsworth',[3] he undermines the very writing that he's exploring. More important, by making literary value the engine of his criticism, Brown cuts off social, cultural and political approaches that could counteract the marginalization that literary history has enforced on late-eighteenth-century writing. In contrast, I want to argue that the cultural significance of this period only emerges if we downplay the aesthetic value judgements that literary history has historically promoted.

As it happens, Brown's position is hard to sustain even on its own terms. Much mid-eighteenth-century poetry is in dialogue with past writers, and this does involve a search for new forms. But that doesn't mean the period is defined by a collective writers' block in which 'major' authors fail to write 'major' works. Leaving aside Brown's aesthetic value judgements and turning to the matter of bulk, it's true that Thomas Gray wrote fewer poems than most other canonical writers but Cowper's poetry is collected in three volumes and his prose works run to five. The standard edition of Gray's letters is three volumes long. Thomson's and Smart's poems are collected in two and six volumes respectively, while Goldsmith can claim to be one of the few – possibly the only – British writer to have produced enduringly popular works in three separate genres (*She Stoops to Conquer, The Vicar of Wakefield* and 'The Deserted Village').

Furthermore a writer such as Cowper, who was the favourite poet of both Jane Austen and Charlotte Brontë, cannot be said to be a frustrated underachiever. To my eyes, Cowper's story is not about artistic unfulfilment. Rather it's about how his work has been erased by the very categories that Brown wants to apply to him. In other words, if Cowper's significance was recognized by writers as different as Austen and Brontë, why was he barely read or taught through the twentieth century? Could it be that the discourse that is meant to preserve his work – literary history – has instead shunted him aside in favour of the subsequent generation? Witness T. S. Eliot claiming, in 1930, that later eighteenth-century poetry is dominated by imitations of Milton that are 'respectable only because Cowper, Thomson, and Edward Young made this line the vehicle for reflection and for observation of nature which prepared the way for Wordsworth'.[4] Is there much difference between this judgement and Brown's contention, over sixty years later, that 'romanticism begins' with Wordsworth's 'productive and self-conscious perfection' of an earlier eighteenth-century form in which 'inner and outer senses alike' are embraced?[5]

Moreover, although Brown acknowledges a relationship between literature and philosophy he does not extend the same welcome to non-literary writing, or to writing that has been denied canonical status: not one of his twelve chapters deals with a female author. His approach also shows the danger of working in a closed system in which texts are included on the basis of predetermined literary judgements. Just as pre-romanticism is often defined, in a circular manner, by examples of pre-romantic texts, so too is Brown's investigation of literary history limited to the texts that literary historians have decided are characteristic of their time.

Brown's immanent (that is, self-enclosed) version of literary history is not the only way to imagine the relationship between writing and period. If the literary text is viewed as a product of social and ideological pressures, then concepts such as generic change are better understood through a cultural history that can reach beyond literariness to include education, gender, class, nationhood, ethnicity. In addition, works claiming literary status should be considered through and alongside modes of representation that use less privileged registers. For instance we lose a valuable interpretive framework if we fail to acknowledge that most of Cowper's poems were enclosed in letters before they were printed for a wider public. Further contextual layers are lost if we ignore the cues that those letters provide to the legal, journalistic and popular cultural debates that preoccupied Cowper and helped to shape his poetry.

## THE 'PRE' OF PRE-ROMANTICISM

My rejection of an immanent literary history ought not to be controversial: new historicism has gone much further over the last thirty years. However my decision to retain the term 'pre-romantic' *does* need explanation. After all, I've already identified it as a problematic relic of the outdated versions of literary history that I'm trying to displace.

Paradoxically, 'pre-romanticism' may be useful precisely because the word is problematic. In particular, its inherent instability might reveal both our need for, and the impossibility of, literary history. After all, literary history is not entirely misguided. Most authors have an awareness of their predecessors and contemporaries, and mapping such connections is a perfectly respectable exercise; indeed it forms part of my own method. However it's a mistake to suppose that these writerly relations form a monolithic whole: rather, they proceed uncertainly and impulsively, and with reference to the scandalous, the popular and the extra-literary, as well as to respectable, critically-approved models. Crucially, it would also be wrong to submit these 'writerly relations' to a rigidly chronological framework. On the contrary, I argue below that although the past proceeds, year by year, in a linear fashion our imaginative engagement with the past is not, and cannot be, sequential.

For me, then, 'pre-romanticism' hints – by its awkwardness – at both the seductions and the difficulties of period-based study. Whether literary historians acknowledge it or not, the term is double-faced and anti-linear in ways that rebound on other literary-historical categories. That is, literary history's teleological thrust demands that writers be placed in an equal and simultaneous relation to the past and the future: they must be seen both to shape what follows and be influenced by what has gone before. However this Janus-faced vision does not match the actual experience of writing. Indeed it produces an ontologically impossible identity because the future to which writers supposedly look is, in fact, invisible to them. Historians know what it looks like (for they have access to what follows) but writers do not. (This is why there can be no such thing as a consciously pre-romantic identity.)

That's not to say that writers don't think about the future: Jerome McGann argues that 'an imagination of the future, of what the future should be, determines both the writing and the reading of the texts we inherit and create'.[6] However we need to distinguish between the imagined futures with which writers may be in dialogue and the actual futures that enfold after their works are published. Although these futures are different, literary history collapses them together, creating a story that is represented (with the benefit of hindsight) as inevitable. What's more, by imagining an active and specific relationship between the present, the past, and the unenacted future, literary history replaces cultural context with after-the-event rationalizations. This is as true of romanticism as it is of pre-romanticism. But as we have seen, the term 'pre-romantic' is additionally challenging because it asks us to read late-eighteenth-century culture in terms of things that had not yet happened. Although this looks like a fundamentally anti-historical approach, one could argue that history is defined by such muddles: after all, we are forever interpreting past events in terms of the ones that followed them, even though by doing so we move still further from the lived experience of the original participants. The 'pre' of 'pre-romanticism' might be useful, therefore, in revealing the impossibility of the very history that the term is trying to articulate.

Eccentrically, then, I value 'pre-romanticism' because the category announces its own incoherence: literary history does better when it acknowledges its instability. By contrast, terms such as 'romanticism' and 'modernism' have become so naturalized that many readers do not question, or even notice, their simplifications and discontinuities. A helpful analogue is provided, here, by discussions of the prefix 'post'. For example Anne McClintock has used Walter Benjamin to reveal the internal contradictions of the 'post' in 'post-colonial'[7] while Kwame Anthony Appiah has asked if the 'post' in 'postcolonial' is the same as the 'post' in 'postmodernism'.[8] Alan Sinfield has toyed with 'post-gay'[9] while Patricia Duncker sceptically examines the possibility of being 'post-gender'.[10] Jonathan Dollimore suggests that in Oscar Wilde the postmodern precedes the modern,[11] and Robert Young has demonstrated the ambiguity of the 'post' in 'poststructuralism'.[12] Building on Young's work, and on Freud's comments on *déjà vu*, Nicholas Royle has theorized 'post-theory'[13] while Francis Fukuyama has declared, infamously, that the western world is (as of 1989) post-historic.[14]

Despite their different agendas, these commentators share an interest in the disciplinary and philosophical implications of temporally-inflected prefixes. When they are placed alongside each other, theorizations of 'post', and my own investigations of 'pre', promote larger speculations about the structures of historical thought. Does our use of these prefixes suggest, for example, that western historical narratives are always, and inevitably, relational? And if so, what forms of blindness and insight are promoted by these habits of thought? More immediately, one could echo Kwame Anthony Appiah by asking why the 'pre' of 'pre-romanticism' is different from the 'pre' of 'pre-colonial' or the 'pre' of 'prehistoric'. Or what of Robert Young's contention that the ambiguities of the 'post' in poststructuralism mean that poststructuralism 'cannot be defined through a certain conceptual content, but only through its insistently deranging pressure'.[15] Following Young, Nicholas Royle connects the 'deranging force'[16] of 'post-theory' to Freud's comments on *déjà vu*. Such comments resemble my argument that the contradictions of 'pre-romanticism' illuminate both our need for, and the impossibility of, definitional categories. In other words, pre-romanticism has its own 'deranging force'. Moreover, *déjà vu* is especially suggestive in relation to pre-romanticism since the latter asks us to believe that romanticism is 'already seen' by pre-romanticism.

There is a danger, here, of using deconstructive language to reinstate or re-legitimate literary history's traditional narratives about the romantic and the pre-romantic. That is not my aim. Instead I want to suggest that Royle's reading of *déjà vu* allows us to recognize the unsettling (Royle would say 'uncanny') characteristics of more than one literary-historical designation. Moreover, as the next section will argue, concepts of pre-romanticism have a formative role in the evolution of the literary-historical genealogies that lead, ultimately, to terms such as 'postmodern' and 'poststructuralist'. Thus, the uncanniness of 'post-theory' may already be implied in the uncanniness of the preromantic.

## IS LITERARY HISTORY LINEAR?

Given that pre-romanticism inhabits one period while looking towards a future one, it is not surprising that many of the writers associated with it are themselves ambiguously situated within linear versions of literary history. Taking Cowper as an instance, this portion of the chapter will explore my contention, above, that 'although the past proceeds, year by year, in a linear fashion our imaginative engagement with the past is not, and cannot be, sequential'. In doing so, I will return to the Gray letter with which I began this introduction. But first I want to look more closely at questions of reception.

I have already noted that Cowper's poetry was prized both by Jane Austen and by her severe critic, Charlotte Brontë. However the characteristics that appeal to Austen are not necessarily the qualities admired by Brontë. Where Austen's Fanny Price uses *The Task* to argue that an ancient avenue of trees should be preserved from the interfering grasp of landscape gardeners, Brontë's Caroline Helstone recites 'The Castaway' during a storm in which 'the wild sea, the drowning mariner, the reluctant ship' are 'realised' in her reading along with 'the heart of the poet' who 'traced a semblance to his own God-abandoned misery in the fate of that man-forsaken sailor'.[17]

If both Brontë and Austen can cite Cowper approvingly, his poetry evidently features a variety of registers; Cowper also has additional moods, notably comedy. However literary historians tend to downplay this versatility. Having gravely examined Cowper's ironic account of growing cucumbers, Donald Davie

10

remarks that although 'the tone of course is humorous' it is 'humorous in a special way'. In fact on closer examination, the extract turns out to be 'comical in parts, but serious in sum'.[18] Cowper's switches between comedy, sententiousness and dramatic pathos evidently disturb Davie by presenting a more complex picture than his literary-historical narrative can accommodate. Indeed Cowper's uncertain canonical status reveals literary history's Procrustean tendencies: to fit in, bits of you may have to be lopped off. And once that happens, your health cannot be guaranteed.

However I think there's something else going on in the Austen and Brontë extracts. Promoting his teleological version of 'preromanticism', Marshall Brown argues that 'Eighteenth-century writers are either romantics or they are not...they cannot be both of their age and of a later one'.[19] Brown is obviously right that an author who lived between 1731 and 1800 would have had problems writing about Queen Victoria's accession – or even her birth. But the relationship between texts and history doesn't only involve the period in which a book is written, it also involves the periods in which that book is read. By remembering this dual, or multiple, focus we discover that although poems tend to be produced in a relatively restricted time and place, they may travel, as Sylvia Plath puts it, 'farther than the words of a classroom teacher or the prescriptions of a doctor; if they are very lucky, farther than a lifetime'.[20]

In a sense, therefore, Austen and Brontë show that writers (or rather, bodies of writing) do inhabit more than one age. Indeed multi-locationism is inevitable once the corporal self is supplemented by a 'textual entity' that can be appropriated by later readers.[21] The writings which provide the raw materials for these re-incarnations remain unchanged: it's the perspective that alters. Thus, even allowing that they are citing different parts of Cowper's *oeuvre*, Austen's *Mansfield Park* (1814) and Brontë's *Shirley* (1849) use the poet to articulate distinct moral and aesthetic visions. As readers, Austen and Brontë are licensed to do as they wish with Cowper: it doesn't matter that their readings partly contradict each other. What's more, almost eighty years after its appearance in *Shirley*, Virginia Woolf is entitled to use 'The Castaway' to satirize masculine self-pity: *To*

*The Lighthouse* (1927) has Mr Ramsay appealing for 'women's sympathy' by murmuring the very lines that thrill Charlotte Brontë's Caroline Helstone.[22]

For early-twenty-first century readers, these versions of Cowper exist alongside each other, and alongside Cowper's letters and memoirs. Each constitutes a form of witness, although they are witnessing, of course, to different things. The challenge is to understand that 'William Cowper' consists of a conglomeration of narratives from more than one period, and that these help determine how we read the words on the page. That's why I have attended to literary-historical categories: whether we like them or not, they condition our interpretations, especially if we are considering figures (such as Cowper) who are now chiefly known through literary history.

Historicist criticism therefore needs a vigilant attention to the time and place of composition, but it also demands an acknowledgement of the other time frames (including our own) in which the text has been read. According to this scheme, words like 'pre-romantic' tell us as much, or more, about the history of criticism than they do about the social fabric from which particular books emerge. However that doesn't mean they can be ignored. On the contrary, once such categories have been articulated (and/or contested) they become intrinsic to the texts they purport to describe.

As a consequence, reading may mobilize more than one imagined past. Looking at 'The Castaway' I might recall – or rather, re-construct – the last time I read the poem; or the first; or both. Brontë, Woolf or Sir Leslie Stephen might come to mind. Pieces of irresistible, though not immediately relevant, knowledge might also come forward: such as Marianne Moore telling Elizabeth Bishop that she didn't mind using the word 'rump' in front of her mother because Mrs Moore would recognize it as a reference to Cowper's pet hare who used to 'swing his rump around' on the poet's Turkish carpet.[23]

Crucially, these associations are unlikely to appear in chronological order, like layers of perfectly-preserved architectural remains. Some may fail to rise to the surface, while those that do will be jumbled together with little immediate recognition of the order in which I acquired them or the order in which they were originally brought into being. So while it might be profitable to replace literary history with a genealogy of receptions, the individual reader is subject to a more unruly set of non-linear associations – a product, if you will, of the unconscious.

It is here that Thomas Gray's mischievous books come into their own as an allegory of the relationship between reading, identity and history. Although Gray is writing during the century that gives birth to literary history – and although his later researches into Norse and early English poetry contribute to this development – the 'hubbub of Tongues' in his youthful letter questions the urge to classify and categorize that powers so much eighteenth-century writing. Instead he imagines a space in which the past can argue with the future as well as vice versa. As such the scene in his study anticipates Gillian Beer's argument that 'no historical period consists only of its present' because 'history is ... less linear than constellatory'.[24]

In this regard, Gray's letter contrasts with its most obvious model, the power struggle between the ancients and the moderns in Jonathan Swift's *The Battle of the Books* (1704). In Swift's satire, classical and contemporary volumes struggle for the highest peak of Parnassus – here represented by control of the royal library. After various inflammatory events, there is an armed conflict in which the books – possessed by the spirits of their authors – engage in appropriately matched hand-to-hand combat: Aristotle aims at Francis Bacon but kills Descartes by mistake, while Virgil exchanges gear with Dryden (his translator) since the latter is dressed in ludicrously over-sized armour – and is too scared, in any case, to do battle.

Swift's story was part of an ongoing debate about classical inheritance versus contemporary excellence.[25] Within the controversy, bodies of writing stood, in part, for the civilizations that produced them. Literary quality was not the only thing at stake: the discussion was also, by implication, about whether the emergent French and British empires could equal their Graeco-Roman models. Given this, it's not surprising that *The Battle of the Books* groups the ancients and the moderns into historical teams. Indeed the satire only works if we accept both that writing should be conceptualized via period, and that periods can and should be compared with each other.

Period based study is not the only way to study literature; nor is it necessarily the best way of being historicist for as we have seen, period labels can suppress distinctions even as they heighten similarities. (Are the 'ancients' – whether Greek or Roman – the same as each other?) However the controversy about the ancients and the moderns is just one instance of a structure of thought that becomes dominant over the course of the long-eighteenth century. Tellingly, for example, the eighteenth century sees the first attempt to place Shakespeare's drama chronologically. Before Edmond Malone's *An attempt to ascertain the order in which the plays attributed to Shakespeare were written* (1778) readers would have attended to style, genre and morality; they would not have assumed, as we do, that *The Tempest* (1611) is the playwright's farewell to the theatre or that *Measure for Measure* (1604) is from the transitional middle period.[26]

Although English literature only became a university subject in the late-nineteenth century, literary journalists and genteel scholars had long since created a culture of period-based literary judgments via books such as Samuel Johnson's *Lives of the English Poets* (1779–81), which compared and classified fifty-two poetic predecessors. By then, Thomas Warton had begun publishing *The History of English Poetry* (1774–81), which is usually seen as England's first extended literary history. As a result of such books, an official canon of English literature was in advanced development by the early-nineteenth century: Marilyn Butler puts its appearance as early as the 1820s–30s.[27]

These developments are vital to my project because one of literary history's early verdicts was the privileging of Wordsworth over his immediate predecessors and contemporaries. Indeed the marginalization of late-eighteenth-century poetry was central to Wordsworth's canonization: after all, canons are defined by their exclusions as much as their inclusions. As a consequence, the mid-nineteenth-century canon is partly formed through its construction of an inferior 'pre-romantic' phase. The creation of 'pre-romanticism' is thus one of literary history's constitutive acts: the decisive downgrading of a relatively recent body of writing confirms the literary scholar's power to judge and define 'periods' as well as individual writers and poems.

Returning to Thomas Gray's letter, it's striking that Gray's books – unlike Swift's – do not struggle along period lines. In

14

fact they do not even define themselves as ancient or modern. Instead, theirs is an individualized battle for space in which Gray's study stands, by implication, for the contents of the writer's mind. Moreover, although the books are competing for attention, conversation is made possible by Gray's anti-chronological and cross-disciplinary shelving, and their jockeying does not preclude trans-historical alliances: for example the Comte de Bussy remarks that Catullus is the only person worth talking to in his vicinity.

More permissive than literary history, Gray's narrative lets writers inhabit several eras simultaneously. This makes for unruliness – hence Locke's remark that 'our owner must have very confused ideas, to jumble us so strangely together'(*CTG* i, 94). But perhaps disorder gives a truer picture than literary history does of the ways in which we process knowledge. For although writers cannot read books that have not yet been written, voices from different parts of the past can and do address each other all the time in the mind: and they do so in a far from orderly way. That's why 'William Cowper' features, via Brontë and Woolf, in the modernist and romantic imaginaries in addition to the literary culture of his own time.

Of course Gray's letter is also appealingly comic: it mocks authorial egos as well as the reductive ways in which books are classified. This mischievousness should warn us against mechanistic theories of history: instead the letter sponsors my wish to combine social and cultural contextualizations with an awareness of how literary history can reduce, rather than enlarge, the significance of certain bodies of writing. I am arguing, not entirely paradoxically, for a more attentive historicism and for a sense of how authors can exist beyond the limits of their immediate period. Literary history works against these aims by being, as it were, both ahistoricist and period-obsessed.

If we challenge the literary-historical paradigm we can give 'pre-romantic poetry' a function beyond the merely preparatory. But it's also important to ask what the category's existence tells us about nineteenth-century culture. Why was Wordsworth preferred to Cowper or Gray? What aspects of 'pre-romantic poetry' were deemed threatening or unappealing by the literary critics who created the canon as part of an exercise in national prestige and educational convenience?

These questions matter because literary history has always fused aesthetic imperatives with political ones. Not content with spending large chunks of the eighteenth century being at war with each other, England and France also clashed over the relative merits of Shakespeare and Corneille. The fact that this took the form of a debate about neo-classicism (Corneille observed the unities of Greek drama while Shakespeare did not) only strengthens my point that literary history evolved through and alongside European competition over trading posts and naval strength.

Why, then, were certain writers co-opted to serve this public agenda while others were found to be marginal or even positively unhealthy? The answer to that question is, to a large degree, the story of this volume: the story, that is, of 'pre-romantic poetry'.

## QUIETING THE HUBBUB

Turning first to practical matters, I want to explain the structure of this book and how I've dealt with my own 'hubbub of Tongues'. For reasons of personal preference, Cowper and Gray bulk large in this study. I have not dealt with James Thomson in detail, partly because of space constraints, and partly because Thomson belongs to an older generation than most of the other writers I touch on. I mention Goldsmith and Collins, although I don't have space to do justice to their range, and I have mostly omitted Burns and Smart since they are represented elsewhere in the *Writers and their Work* series.

One of my main concerns has been to restore women to mid- and late-eighteenth poetry – they're only absent from this chapter because I've been analysing the construction of a canon from which they were always already excluded. However subsequent chapters will discuss work by Mary Leapor, Priscilla Pointon, Ann Yearsley, amongst others. Although my focus is on pre-romantic writing, I also discuss earlier poets (especially Alexander Pope) and later ones (particularly Wordsworth and Keats): this seems the best way of conveying the shifts of poetic register that occur from the late-seventeenth-century through to the early-eighteenth-century.

Instead of organizing the analysis via author I use the formal and institutional structures of mid-eighteenth-century poetry to ask why the poetic structures of the mid-century are so compelling for the writers of the period yet so baffling to modern readers. But rather than looking at form for the sake of form, the book investigates the cultural work that is done by a selection of key discourses. Of various available formations, I have chosen patronage, occasional poetry, and the pastoral: these make up my remaining chapters. By emphasizing the cultural burden of poetry, and its organization as a cultural apparatus, I am able to argue that it's the changing institutional status of poetry (rather than any intrinsically 'literary' qualities) that accounts for the varying reputations of poets such as Cowper and Gray on the one hand and Wordsworth and Coleridge on the other. This not only avoids the more reductive aspects of 'pre-romantic' classifications, it also allows us to see that these terms have arisen so as to patrol the limits of 'romantic' writing. Moreover, post-romantic literary theory has occluded the degree to which all poetry – not just that of the eighteenth century – is implicated in social and economic factors. By stressing that insight we may uncover the continuity between eighteenth-century patronage networks and our current culture of 'writers in residence'.

As this last point suggests – and as my introduction indicates – pre-romantic poetry ought to engage a wider audience than students and scholars of the eighteenth century. It's not only that this writing deserves to be better known (although that's certainly true), it's also that its neglect, and the reasons for its neglect, tell us important things about the processes of categorization and canonization that inform the writing of literary history – processes that continue to condition the production of art, academic criticism and literary journalism.

# 2

# Poetry and Patronage

One of the more long-awaited social highlights of 1791 came from Elizabeth Montagu, the so-called 'Queen of the Bluestockings'. Having spent ten years decorating the Portman Square mansion that she built after her husband's death, Montagu threw a breakfast party for 'a numerous and splendid company of the Nobility, Foreign Ambassadours, illustrious Travellers, and Persons of Distinction'.[1] With its James Stuart design and Angelica Kauffman murals, the house bore witness to Montagu's importance as a patron, particularly of gifted women.

Those of us who have laboured at home improvement for almost as long (although with rather less success) can only marvel at Montagu's dedication to the house beautiful. Our excuse will have to be our relative lack of resources. Having expertly managed her husband's business affairs while he was alive, Montagu inherited sole control of an estate that yielded an income of between £7,000 and £10,000 a year – enough to build and decorate the house without borrowing any money.[2] This combination of wealth, artistic taste and social standing made Montagu an invaluable, if somewhat high-handed, contact for aspiring writers, intellectuals and politicians.

Even if he had been invited (which he wasn't), it's unlikely that William Cowper would have attended Montagu's opening. After the 1763 mental breakdown that led to his first suicide attempt, Cowper moved from London to an asylum in St Albans. Settling subsequently in Buckinghamshire, he walked, gardened, and wrote poetry that praised rural retirement at the expense of urban dissipation. (As one of his most famous lines put it, 'God made the country, and man made the town' (*PWC* ii, 136).) His accompanying self-portraits emphasized modesty, pain, isolation, and passivity; typical poems show him identifying with grasshoppers (*PWC* i, 256) and hares (*PWC* ii, 171), as well as with the 'stricken deer' that finds itself separated from the herd and pierced with arrows from the hunt (*PWC* ii, 165–6).

Cowper's sequestered life forms the surface pattern of his most influential poem, *The Task* (1785), which uses countryside vignettes to meditate on religion, culture and politics. Many of Cowper's shorter poems also celebrate rural domesticity. If we turn the tapestry over, however, we find that these non-metropolitan scenes are underpinned by knotted threads of supplication and ambition. When untied, the skeins lead to London, and to a series of patrons and failed patrons, including Elizabeth Montagu. Indeed there is a direct connection between Montagu's carefully-crafted décor and the enterprise which Cowper saw as the culmination of his poetic career: his monumental blank verse translation of the *Iliad* and the *Odyssey*.

Given Cowper's penchant for animal fables, it's apt that his and Montagu's encounter can be shaped into a story about swans, peacocks and moles, as well as country estates and tapestry workers. In putting the tale together, I mean to argue that Cowper's cultural significance cannot be separated from the economic foundations of his work. This in turn will set up my next chapter, which looks at occasional poetry. In the present chapter, though, I want to concentrate on the spoken and unspoken contracts through which literary patronage operated – or failed to operate – in the late-eighteenth century. Though the story is selective, it is not unrepresentative.


## 'CHATTELS OF LEISURE AND EASE'

Long before its official opening, it was known that Elizabeth Montagu's London house would contain a room decorated entirely with feathers. (This is where the swans and peacocks will come in.) In 1788 – three years before the decorations were complete – Cowper wrote a poem praising Montagu's feather hangings. He did so at the behest of his cousin and benefactress, Lady Hesketh. Hesketh hoped to join what she called Mrs Montagu's 'Academy' and she felt that Cowper, who had gained unexpected fame after the 1785 publication of *The Task*, was well-placed to catch Montagu's eye.

Although Montagu had written an important study of Shakespeare, she was best known as a patron and hostess. She gave financial support to – amongst others – the poet and classical scholar Elizabeth Carter, the poets Anna Williams and James Woodhouse, and the novelists Sarah Fielding and Sarah Scott. (Scott was also her sister.) Montagu's salons – which had begun by 1750 – were so famous that Richard Samuel had painted her, around 1775, as one of the 'Nine Living Muses of Great Britain'. As well as Angelica Kauffman and Elizabeth Carter, other 'Muses' accredited to Britain by Samuel included the historian Catherine Macaulay, the poets Anna Barbauld and Hannah More, and the novelist Charlotte Lennox.[3] Montagu was much less artistically productive than the other women in the painting but her financial muscle was enormous. This is presumably why Samuels identifies her as the group's chief Muse – a move that neatly illustrates culture's dependence on cash.

Cowper's cousin, Lady Hesketh, was fairly comfortably off: she did not need Montagu's money. And nor was she seeking artistic advancement. But like many lively and socially-determined women, Hesketh recognized the cultural value of Montagu's circle: to be a bluestocking was to be witty and worthy of notice. It was not, however, to be a political radical. Despite its subsequent associations, 'bluestocking' was initially used of both women and men; and though its gender-specific meaning had emerged by the last decade of the eighteenth century, blue-stocking women were still more likely to be learned than revolutionary. Montagu's parties complemented rather than replaced existing middle-class structures, and younger bluestockings, such as Hannah More, were to be among the most fervent of Mary Wollstonecraft's opponents. As a confirmed Tory, Hesketh would have seen much to emulate and little to deride in Montagu's gatherings.

Hesketh knew that Cowper would do what he could to advance her claims. As Harriot Cowper, she and her sister Theadora had known the poet from youth. The family connection was strengthened when William studied law in London; for three years he was barely out of his uncle's town house, where poetry was much discussed (*LWC* ii, 428, 523). Religious disagreements later placed a chill between the cousins, and when Hesketh resumed contact in late 1785 it was after a break of eighteen years. However from then on she was one of Cowper's most important correspondents; their letters illustrate a mutual affection that was strengthened by Cowper's need to feel imbedded in supportive family structures. This in itself would have been a reason for Cowper to smooth his friend's entry to Montagu's 'Academy'. But Hesketh's support wasn't just emotional, it was also fiscal.

Although born to genteel habits, Cowper was financially insecure. His inheritance was small and his law studies had been less than committed. Though his family controlled lucrative government sinecures, the young Cowper could not bring himself to appear before the parliamentary committee that would have granted him his desired office; the resultant panic both produced, and was a symptom of, his 1763 breakdown and suicide attempt.[4] Although he recovered, there would be further collapses in 1773, 1786 and 1794, and he was left unable to pursue a profession. After his release from the asylum, he spent a year's allowance of cash in three months. Retrenching, he gave up private chambers to lodge with a clergyman's family in Huntingdon. The woman of the house, Mary Unwin, persuaded her husband to halve Cowper's rent, and when the Reverend Unwin died nineteenth months later, Cowper stayed on as Mrs Unwin's platonic friend. They lived together – unmarried and without a sexual relationship – for over thirty years, until Unwin's death in 1796.

Even though their relationship had been founded on a mutual attachment to evangelical Christianity, Cowper and Unwin were subject to gossip when they moved from Huntingdon to Olney in 1767. Unwed couples weren't supposed to share a house (especially if they were respectable) so it's hardly surprising that the widow and the poet were hit by unkind speculation. The scandalmongering was perhaps an attempt to control a relationship that had exceeded – or failed to meet? – society's approved models for how men and women should behave together. Even now, scholars have yet to trace the arrangement's full implications for friendship, marriage and the family. But for my present purposes, the relationship's most interesting feature is that, having construed Mary Unwin as a replacement for the mother that he had lost when he was six,

Cowper became financially, as well as emotionally, reliant on her. There's a certain logic here, for parental love is often figured through cash transactions. But since Unwin was only seven years older than Cowper, casual observers would have read the alliance as a quasi-marriage; and in those terms, it was unseemly (though hardly unprecedented) for the male partner to rely financially on the female. Of course if they had been married, Unwin's property would have passed to Cowper. By remaining single, the poet rejected the legal and sexual powers that would have confirmed his adult masculinity, and thus offset his financial dependence. In any case, Mary Unwin's daughter – who resented what she saw as Cowper's usurpation of her father's role – said that her mother had contributed £1,800 to the poet's upkeep.[5]

As we've seen, Cowper and Lady Hesketh resumed contact after Cowper's second book of poems was published. Like its predecessor, this volume had been printed at the publisher's expense (who thus retained the copyright). Cowper, as was perhaps fitting for a gentleman, gained no money from the sales. He did, though, have a small income from stocks and from the rent of his former chambers in the Inner Temple. These, together with a family annuity, would have yielded just over £40 a year. An old legal friend, Joseph Hill, administered and supplemented Cowper's stock. Although Hill's subsidies brought the poet's income to £100 per annum this was barely enough to live respectably, even in the country, and was certainly insufficient for someone who kept a manservant and was particular about his dress. No wonder Susanna Unwin felt that her mother was offsetting Cowper's expenses.

Be that as it may, Harriot Hesketh sensed that Cowper's circumstances could be further enhanced. After her 1786 visit to Olney, she arranged for Cowper and Unwin to move to a larger house where they would have increased privacy and a better social circle. The move had been mooted earlier, but the house was unfurnished and the couple could not afford to equip it. Since it had been her father who gave Cowper the sinecure that led to his 1763 breakdown, Hesketh was continuing a family tradition when she sent her cousin books, clothes, wine, and furniture for the new residence. Hesketh also forwarded gifts from an unnamed donor, probably her sister Theadora (with whom Cowper had had an abortive courtship thirty years before). These included an annuity of £50 a year, food parcels and, significantly, a writing desk.

Our knowledge of these presents comes from the witty, graceful letters in which Cowper acknowledges them. However Gray's gratitude isn't merely a topic within the letters, it is also the impetus behind them. Lacking the means to buy his cousin gifts, Cowper gives Hesketh – and his other benefactors – personally-tailored linguistic offerings. Poems are intrinsic to this exchange since many of Cowper's shorter pieces were enclosed in letters to benefactors; what's more, these poems often express the donor's generosity and/or the beneficiary's gratitude.

The next section of this chapter will explore the pecuniary implications of Cowper's poem about Elizabeth Montagu's feather room. But first I want to look at the pieces immediately preceding the Montagu poem in the standard edition of Cowper's works. Both were enclosed in letters to Harriot Hesketh; they are 'Benefactions. A Poem in Shenstone's Manner Address'd to my Dear Coz, April 14, 1788' and 'Gratitude. Addressed to Lady Hesketh'. The second poem is a rewrite of the first in which slightly risqué intimacy is replaced by public discretion. The title change, by which 'my Dear Coz' becomes 'Lady Hesketh', announces this increased gravity; indeed Cowper regretted sending the earlier text to another correspondent, Mrs King, and told her to commit it 'to the flames' as he was ashamed of it (LWC iii, 358).

And shameful the piece surely is, for it refers – please don't be shocked – to the poet's bottom. This questionable body part has the good fortune to rest in a generously upholstered chair which fits the 'Sitter, both Bottom and Back'. The poem also features Cowper's cap and ribbon, his carpet, his dressing table, the mirror in which he shaves, his book shelves, his china service and the cabinet that contains it, his study curtains, the kitchen range, a beer barrel, plus 'Bedding and Beds above stairs, / With other things not to be named'. Predictably, each of these items derives from Hesketh, and Cowper's challenge is to enumerate the gifts appreciatively without becoming heavy-handed. His success in doing so is a tribute to the mock-heroic poise with which he can tell 'ye Knights of the Boot' not to mess

23

with 'These Carpets so soft to the foot' (*PWC* iii, 19–20). Significantly, though, the revised poem ('Gratitude') is eight lines shorter: Cowper cuts the kitchen and beer barrel references, rewrites the chair section to avoid mentioning anything stronger than an elbow, takes the word 'dirt' from the third stanza, and removes his oddly loaded allusion to bed linen and 'other things not to be named'.

Cowper sent Hesketh the new version, noting that it was 'less witty but more decent' than his first attempt (*LWC* iii, 355). These revisions show how poetic register can follow, and serve, the dictates of polite conversation: Cowper's benefactor may be his 'Dear Coz' but as 'Lady Hesketh' she deserves respect as well as affection. Significantly, though, the shift to a more decorous tone also changes the poem's construction of authorship. The revised version ends with Cowper encircled by status symbols:

> Thus compass'd about with the Goods
> And Chattels of leisure and ease
> I indulge my poetical moods
> In many such fancies as these.

> (*PWC* iii, 22)

The poem bespeaks Cowper's status as gentleman-writer, not just because it surrounds him with expensive objects but also – and more importantly – because the poem is itself a product of the 'leisure and ease' that is Hesketh's real gift.

By representing his poems as indulgences derived from 'moods' and 'fancies', Cowper distances himself from hack writers who overproduce because they're being paid by the line. Of course Cowper can afford to sound superior: he has been rewarded in advance, and on rather generous terms. But then class smugness is another of Hesketh's benefactions, not least because it's likely to encourage further genteel productions. Cowper notes as much when praising Hesketh's bookcase, in which

> *My* poems enchanted I view,
> And hope in due time to behold
> *My* Iliad and Odyssey too.
> (*PWC* iii, 22; emphasis in Cowper's text.)

This refers to Cowper's projected translation of Homer, which Hesketh tirelessly promoted. 'Benefactions' and 'Gratitude' can therefore be seen as down payments in advance of his next major work.

Although both versions of the poem mention the Homer translation, Cowper's first rendering ('Benefactions') doesn't have the 'Chattels of leisure and ease' section quoted above. Instead it closes with the poet telling himself to while away his cousin's absence by bursting into 'poetical fire'. Since he is 'athirst' for 'true glory' it is his job

> In high-flying ditty to rise
> On feathers renown'd from the first
> For bearing a Goose to the skies.
>
> (*PWC* iii, 20)

This is both funnier and less pretentious than the revised version. Instead of a gentleman-poet contemplating a brand-new collection of Georgian furniture, we have a mock-heroic ditty-maker who wafts his way to Parnassus on goose feathers. The feathers, of course, are a material prerequisite for poetic immortality: Cowper is writing with the quills that they provide. But by taking ownership of the feathers, the poet identifies himself as a goose – in the alternative sense of a foolish person.[6]

Taken as a whole, Cowper's revisions emphasize both his and his patron's decorum. Cowper is no longer a goose, and his bottom disappears from view; instead we have a refined gentleman whose polish reflects well upon his cousin. Moreover, the 'poetical moods' that produce Cowper's poetry are acknowledged as coming from Hesketh's largesse. This contrasts with Cowper's portrait-of-the-artist-as-a-goose, partly because the revised version is more genteel, but also because the goose controls its own destiny: self-deprecating though it is, the image shows Cowper ascending without his cousin's help. By comparison, it is hard to read Cowper's account of the 'Chattels of leisure and ease' without reflecting that he himself may be the ultimate 'Chattel', and that he embraces the role with vigour.

## 'ALL TRIBES BESIDE OF INDIAN NAME'

'Benefactions' and 'Gratitude' aren't Cowper's only offerings to Hesketh. Another poem, 'To my Dearest Cousin on her Removal of us From Silver End, to Weston' celebrates Cowper and Unwin's relocation from 'infant-throng'd, thief-harb'ring' Olney to a 'neat Mansion furnish'd by her [Harriot's] care'. Somewhat implausibly, the piece compares this move to Lot's escape from Sodom, with Hesketh descending from 'proud Hyde-Park' to conduct them to a home (less than two miles away) in which 'Rustics who can only gape and gaze' have been replaced by 'Good neighbourhood with all its social sweets' (*PWC* iii, 5).

'Good neighbourhood', of course, is a synonym for the right class of person; and Cowper did indeed write several pieces for his new neighbours, the Throckmortons, who let him range freely over their considerable estate. Cowper's poem about Elizabeth Montagu's feather room makes a similar bid for breeding and intellect. However the feather poem shows Cowper acting in the interests of Lady Hesketh's social life, not his own. By doing for Hesketh what Hesketh has done for him, the poem lets Cowper thank his cousin for her emotional and material support; but it also has implications for his own income.

'On Mrs Montagu's Feather-Hangings' begins by briskly asserting that 'The Birds put off their ev'ry hue / To grace a Room for Montagu'. The birds, we note, are active: they voluntarily divest themselves of their colourful plumage. This is fortunate given that Cowper was a long-standing opponent of blood sports. His portrayal of himself as a 'stricken deer' is only the most famous of the many passages where he condemns the savagery of huntsmen. Also apposite are his *tour-de-force* letter about a fox hunt that ended in his garden (*LWC* iii, 117–20), his denunciation of hare-coursing in Book III of *The Task* (*PWC* ii, 170–1) and the same poem's long, philosophical attack on man's abuse of animals (*PWC* ii, 245–53). This last instance includes the lines,

> I would not enter on my list of friends
> (Though grac'd with polish'd manners and fine sense
> Yet wanting sensibility) the man
> Who needlessly sets foot upon a worm.

> (*PWC,* ii, 251)

26

In the feather poem, however, Cowper chooses to identify with Montagu's artistic effects rather than with the creatures that form her raw materials.

The birds in the poem are both native and foreign. First the peacock 'sends his heav'nly dyes'. The pheasant, the cock and the swan follow suit, each paying Montagu the tribute of its feathers. Then,

> All tribes beside of Indian name
> That glossy shine or vivid flame,
> Where rises, and where sets the day,
> Whate'er they boast of rich and gay
> Contribute to the gorgeous plan,
> Proud to advance it all they can.

These unnamed exotics come from both ends of the earth ('Where rises, and where sets the day') and they, too, are eager to play a part in Montagu's scheme. The birds offer their plumage so that it can be 'screen'd from ev'ry storm that blows'. The feathers will therefore remain 'for ever new, / Safe with protecting Montagu' (*PWC* iii, 23).

When the birds voluntarily release their plumage into Montagu's protection, they not only exonerate the hunters who shoot them, they also obscure the extent to which feather-trafficking denuded overseas communities. Certain feathers were rare, and the feather trade could be savage. Much later, Virginia Woolf would juxtapose a Regent Street lady pausing before a 'display of egret plumes, artfully arranged' with a 'blazing South American landscape' in which a bird is 'tightly held in one hand while another hand pierces the eyeballs with a feather'; this decoy bird will reel around the sky, attracting nesting birds to be shot while their unfed offspring 'rot where they sit'. By exposing the alliance between cruelty and capitalism, Woolf forces her reader to wonder if these 'fantastically lovely' feathers should really be taken as 'the natural adornment of spirited and fastidious life, the very symbols of pride and distinction'.[7]

Although Woolf is writing in 1920, her strictures can be applied, in their essence, to earlier stages in the feather trade. The bird in Woolf's essay, the egret, was common in eighteenth-century headgear. Some accounts suggest that the ostrich was hunted to virtual extinction in the eighteenth century, so great was the demand for its plumage; later, the birds would be farmed in colonial outposts in Southern Africa, and in North and South America. In any case, the image of a bird blinded by its own feather graphically conveys the circular relationship between commodities, consumers, and the consumed. As well as being mutilated by the very thing that has attracted the hunters' attention, the bird is converted, before death, into an object: it ceases to exist except as a collection of plumes to be bought and sold. Simultaneously, the sightless bird comments on the ethical blindness of both the hunter and the Regent Street lady.

Cowper's poem betrays a similar failure of vision. By having the birds turn themselves over to Montagu's care, the piece echoes the imperialist habit of justifying exploitation via a language of 'protection'. Paternalism and exploitation are similarly fused in a poem from earlier in the century, Alexander Pope's *Windsor Forest* (1713), which provides a helpful template for thinking about poetry's implication in commodity culture.[8] Pope's poem depicts world peace as the inevitable consequence of Britain's control of the seas. Here Father Thames compares his sway to that of rival rivers:

> Let *Volga's* Banks with Iron Squadrons shine,
> And Groves of Lances glitter on the *Rhine*,
> Let barb'rous *Ganges* arm a servile Train;
> Be mine the Blessings of a peaceful Reign.

> (*PAP* 208)

The trees of Windsor Forest maintain the Thames's power over other waterways because, as ships, they enforce Britain's trading superiority:

> Let *India* boast her Plants, nor envy we
> The weeping Amber or the balmy Tree,
> While by our Oaks the precious Loads are born,
> And Realms commanded which those Trees adorn.

> (*PAP* 196)

However the logic of empire demands that mercantile domination be seen to benefit the people whose natural resources are being stripped. Thus:

The Time shall come, when free as Seas or Wind
Unbounded *Thames* shall flow for all Mankind,

. . . . . .

Earth's distant Ends our Glory shall behold,
And the new World launch forth to seek the Old.
Then Ships of uncouth Form shall stem the Tyde,
And Feather'd People crowd my wealthy Side,
And naked Youths and painted Chiefs admire
Our Speech, our Colour, and our strange Attire!
Oh stretch thy Reign, fair *Peace!* from Shore to Shore,
'Till Conquest cease, and Slav'ry be no more;
'Till the freed *Indians* in their native Groves
Reap their own Fruits, and woo their Sable Loves.

*(PAP* 209–10)

Slavery and conquest will end, that is, when Britannia rules the waves.

Laura Brown's classic reading argues that the poem creates this vision of global peace by displacing imperial violence onto an alternative target – namely the birds of Windsor Forest.[9] Hoards of partridges, pheasants, doves, woodcocks, lapwings and larks are lyrically despatched in lines 93–134 of the poem. The 'feather'd people' who pay homage to London in the above extract are therefore shadowed by the feathered creatures who 'fall, and leave their little Lives in Air' when they are shot by 'slaught'ring Guns' *(PAP* 199–200). It's a stunning interpretation, not least because it exposes the destructive power of a standard rustic scene (the hunt), and knits that power into a broader argument about poetry's role in creating and sustaining an imperial rhetoric.

Brown's reading sheds further light on Cowper's poem. The equivalence that Brown draws between hunted birds and 'feather'd people', makes Cowper's 'tribes...of Indian name' seem potently ambiguous. What does it mean for the poet to imagine these birds as 'tribes'? Is he alluding to birds – or to people? The literal reference, obviously, is to birds, but the usage activates other possibilities, especially if we consider the many seventeenth- and eighteenth-century texts in which native peoples are represented through or alongside plumage. These literary and visual representations are sometimes so insistent that the feathers and the person seem to fuse into one.[10] Indeed this fusion was made literal, in a grotesquely parodic form, through the practice of tarring and feathering runaway slaves.

I don't mean that Cowper is consciously using birds as a metaphor for people (although Montagu may be). However I do think that his poem draws on a complex set of associations in which exploitative trading relations produce a commodified and exoticized version of 'native' cultures. This can be inferred both from the analogous example of *Windsor Forest*, and from Cowper's portraits of the 'gentle savage' Omai (*PWC* ii, 133). Having picked Omai up on a South Pacific island, Tobias Furneaux (who was travelling with Captain James Cook) brought the young man to England in 1774, where he became a social celebrity before being returned home on Cook's next voyage; Cowper writes about Omai in *The Task*, and in several letters.

Omai's divided identity – or rather, the divisions that were forced on him by English observers – can be inferred from Joshua Reynolds's decision to paint him in an odd mixture of classical and oriental garb even though he had appeared at court in fashionable Western clothes.[11] For his part, Cowper presented Omai as a childlike outsider with natural charm. Cowper never met him so his version is derived from Cook's journals, from newspaper accounts of Omai, and from prior constructions of the noble savage. (A figure that went back at least as far as the Renaissance.) For my present purposes I'm particularly interested in the way that Cowper links Omai to Britain's trading activities. Having drawn a pathetic picture of Omai's life back in the Society Islands, Cowper notes that the young man would never again see England because there were no commodities in his homeland to draw back English ships. The implication is that Omai is himself a sort of failed commodity. This is reinforced by the way that Cowper and Cook surround him with markers of 'natural' exoticism. Cowper pictures him in his 'homestall thatch'd with leaves' among his 'cocoas and bananas, palms and yams' (*PWC* ii, 133).

As it happens, Elizabeth Montagu also read Captain Cook's journals; ironically, she was sickened by what she saw as Cook's obsessive interest in 'sea fowl'.[12] (Why do the words 'pot', 'kettle' and 'black' spring to mind?) In any case, Montagu, Pope and Cowper can be seen to share their culture's growing investment in the idea of empire. What's more, Cowper's poem for Mrs Montagu both draws attention to – and is itself a product of – Britain's exploitation of non-metropolitan communities. By praising the feather room, Cowper celebrates Montagu's ability to gather expensive imports, and to arrange them in 'exotic' ways.[13] Indeed on the bluntest of levels, he's complimenting her spending power, for though some of the feathers were gathered by friends, Montagu's room was conceived – like the rest of her house – as a statement of conspicuous consumption.[14]

## 'THE MOLE, THE MINER OF THE SOIL'

Although Montagu and Cowper used feathers to create a sense of otherness, 'Indian' chiefs are not the only people for whom plumage is a sign of rank. Since the fourteenth century, the emblem of the Prince of Wales has been three ostrich plumes. Egret, ostrich and other feathers feature in many English coats of arms,[15] and they were also a staple of eighteenth-century women's fashion – as can be seen from numerous portraits by Thomas Gainsborough and Sir Joshua Reynolds. No arbitrary whim, then, the feather room advertised Montagu's entitlement to respect on the multiple grounds of birth, marriage, wealth and gender.[16] Crucially, though, it also indicated her status as a writer and patron; for a room of feathers was also a room full of writing implements.

Earlier in this chapter, I looked at a poem in which Cowper pictures himself rising to the skies on goose feathers: rising, that is, on the quills that the geese provide. Given the person he's addressing, it's not surprising that Cowper recycles this play on feathers, quills and writing in the Montagu poem. Having introduced the birds and their plumage, Cowper shows various aspects of the creative temperament seeking refuge with 'the same Patroness' as the birds:

> All these to Montagu's repair
> Ambitious of a shelter there;
> There, Genius, Learning, Fancy, Wit,
> Their ruffled plumage, calm, refit
> (For stormy troubles loudest roar
> Around their flight who highest soar)

31

And in Her eye, and by Her aid
Shine safe, without a fear to fade.

(*PWC* iii, 23-4)

In the earlier poem, Cowper was an absurd goose-like figure, but here writers are shown as noble aspirants whose difficulties increase the higher they fly. Montagu, though, will offer these troubled figures the same protection she extends to storm-tossed birds.

By now the piece seems to have moved from Lady Hesketh's wishes to Cowper's. Hesketh was neither needy nor a poet, whereas Cowper was both; moreover, he often used storms as metaphors for his mental upheavals. This shift is confirmed by the poem's close, which shows Montagu combining forces with Phœbus Apollo, the god of poetry.

She thus maintains divided sway
With yon bright Regent of the day,
The Plume and the Poet both we know
Their lustre to his influence owe,
And, She the works of Phœbus aiding
Both Poet saves and Plume from fading.

(*PWC* iii, 24)

As sun-god, Phœbus is the 'bright Regent of the day' who inspires poets and gives sheen to birds. Montagu matches his work by sheltering poets and by protecting the birds' feathers from decay. This compliment can hardly be applied to Lady Hesketh's wish to join the bluestocking circle; it seems more like an appeal from Cowper to a potential patron. And as it turns out, Cowper isn't only promoting Lady Hesketh's claims. He is also thinking about his forthcoming Homer translation.

Having failed to make money from his previous books, Cowper wanted to capitalize on his newly-acquired fame by publishing his version of the *Iliad* and the *Odyssey* by subscription. That is: copies would be assigned, in advance, to subscribers who undertook to buy the book. A large subscription list would yield a lump sum for the author once the publisher had deducted costs and an agreed percentage of the profits; however a book could not go to press until it had enough takers. Paradoxically, these strictures made subscription publishing attractive to both untried and well-established writers. Famous authors could turn their existing success into a wide subscription base, while new writers could secure a publisher provided they or their patrons could collect enough subscribers.

Cowper fell between these two positions. Although he was a successful writer, his rural retirement cut him off from well-to-do donors. Like many subscription ventures, the Homer translation was pitched at the upper end of the trade: it was available on fine paper for three guineas and on ordinary paper for two. Therefore Cowper needed Hesketh and his other contacts to gather names on his behalf – and so much the better if they were distinguished names. Aristocrats and noted cultural figures would draw other backers in, thus boosting the writer's profits; they also lent status to the enterprise, removing it from the taint of Grub Street.

It isn't surprising, then, to find Cowper rejoicing that his 'Dearest Coz' has received a note from their quarry: 'It may be a good thing to have caught a *Lady* of Mrs. Montagu's eminence in literary accomplishments and of her influence in the literary world, by *the right ear*. My subscription perhaps may feel the benefit of it' (*LWC* iii, 159; emphasis in the original). Nor is it odd that he ponders whether the poem should appear in a widely-read newspaper or the *Gentlemen's Magazine*; he opts for the latter because 'a Compliment paid in a Magazine [is] twice as good as the same Compliment would be in a Newspaper' (*LWC* iii, 161–2). Sending a fair copy to Hesketh in advance of publication, Cowper tells her to 'exhibit away to Right and Left as fast as possible. You will have 5 weeks complete for the exercise of your distributory function' (*LWC* iii, 167). But two months later, he remarks that 'it seemeth that we shall never by any management make a deep impression on Mrs. Montagu. Persons who have been so long accustom'd to praise, become proof against it' (*LWC* iii, 202).

This is a pretty accurate estimate of Montagu's character. However I'm less interested in Cowper's success or otherwise than in the way that his Montagu poem commodifies writing. Like *Windsor Forest*, Cowper's feather poem represents social power in terms of an institution's control over expensive imports, with Montagu performing on a small scale what Britain's ships do in Pope's work. But by equating imported feathers with writers, Cowper allows the inference that poetry is itself a product to be bought and sold.

This insight illuminates Montagu's entire enterprise, not just her dealings with Cowper. For Montagu was indeed an institution, and not only because of her work as a literary and social gatekeeper. Long before her husband's death, Montagu managed extensive properties in Yorkshire, Northumberland and Berkshire, plus a London town house; she subsequently increased these holdings until she could boast, in 1783, of having over five hundred men working for her in Yorkshire alone.[17] Montagu's patronage of the arts is therefore under-written by her commercial function: indeed industry and the humanities come together, through her, in ways that anticipate subsequent forms of arts philanthropy.

As a further aside, we might note that relatively little of Montagu's fortune came from agriculture. Most of it derived from coal mines – hence her observation that the 'naiads' of her Northumberland estate 'were dirty with... coal keels' while 'the dryads' tresses [were] torn and dishevelled with the rough blasts of Boreas'. (In other words, her waterways were soiled from coal barges and her woods were subjected to the rough north wind.) These remarks illuminate the representational shifts produced by late-eighteenth-century Britain's lurch from agriculture to manufacturing industry: the 'naiads' of the pastoral persist, but mostly as the ironic or sentimental residue of another kind of economy. For as Montagu added, coal might be filthy but 'it was a goodly heritage, and made a decent figure when it arrived at the shop of Hoare & Co. in Fleet Street'.[18]

As an advocate of rural retirement, Cowper had mixed feelings about trade (which he associated with London). Although he saw trading vigour as God's reward for national virtue, he was suspicious of the luxury produced by 'profusion' (*PWC* ii, 153–60). And like his admirer Jane Austen, he read landscapes, and those who altered them, in moral terms. Book I of *The Task* compares 'the mole, the miner of the soil' to landowners who turned their estates over to mineral extraction:

> [The mole] not unlike the great ones of mankind,
> Disfigures earth, and plotting in the dark
> Toils much to earn a monumental pile,
> That may record the mischiefs he has done.

> (*PWC* ii, 124)

It would be interesting to know what Elizabeth Montagu thought of these lines. While not directed at her, they certainly cast trade in a different light to that shown by the feather poem. Even so, Cowper's perspective remains genteel: although he is scathing about slag heaps, he's more concerned about the defaced view than the men who work below the surface. Indeed by comparing landowners – rather than miners – to moles, Cowper erases the people who do the actual work.[19]

The mole that burrows blindly in the dark bears little resemblance to the multicoloured bird that glistens in the sun. The first digs sightlessly through earth while the other flies heavenward. The contrast says much about Cowper's ability to project social and moral meanings onto nature. But we might also take the mole as a symptom of the manual labour that is otherwise suppressed or misrepresented in Cowper's work. As such, the mole makes manifest the work that (almost literally) under-writes Elizabeth Montagu's patronage of the arts – the labour that tunnels its way under her mock-heroic vocabulary and that enables her to make a room out of feathers. (Feathers that another woman spent eight years sewing onto tapestries until her mistress intimated that she would die from her efforts and be carried to the next world on the plumage that eventually surrounded her even as she slept.)[20]

By extension, one could argue that it wouldn't be possible to write, distribute or read poetry without other people's unseen labour: the feather room needs the mole's tunnel. This is hardly a new insight, but it does have implications for how we think about the business of writing (and I use the word 'business' advisedly). Accordingly, the rest of this chapter will explore the economic implications of Cowper's status as a gentleman-poet. What sort of trading relations does his work establish? How do these affect the way we think about eighteenth-century poetry? And where do working-class writers fit into this picture?

### 'THE HERRINGS ARE REMARKABLY FINE'

I've looked at Cowper's encounter with Montagu because it exemplifies his pragmatic approach to literary creativity. Similar preoccupations occur in his letters from 1785–91 which return, constantly, to the number and status of the subscribers to his Homer translation. Besides Montagu, Cowper and his contacts pursued (with varying degrees of success) Horace Walpole, the Lord Chancellor Edward Thurlow, William Wilberforce, the Universities of Oxford and Cambridge, several earls, and 'upward of thirty Right Honourable names'.[21] What's more, Cowper's letters – like the feather poem – often turn on trading analogies. Take this 1779 note to his friend and benefactor, Joseph Hill:

> The News Paper informs me of the Arrival of the Jamaica Fleet. I hope it imports some Pine Apple Plants for Me. I have a good Frame & a Good Bed prepared to receive them. I send you annex'd, a Fable in which the Pine Apple makes a Figure, & shall be glad if you Like the Taste of it. – 2 Pairs of Soals with Shrimps which arrived last Night, demand my Acknowledgments. (*LWC* i, 305)

Here Cowper links the movements of Britain's merchant navy to his gardening activities. He then offers his poem, 'The Pine Apple & the Bee', as a literary equivalent of Hill's food parcel: the 'Taste' of his pineapple echoes the more tangible flavour of Hill's 'Soals with Shrimps'.

The more the letter goes on, the more the arrangement is revealed as a well-subsidized form of barter. Having thanked Hill for his shrimps, Cowper adds, 'You have heard that when Arion performed upon the Harp the Fish followed him. I really have no Design to Fiddle you out of more Fish, but if you should Esteem my Verses worthy of such a Price, though I shall never be so renown'd as he was, I shall think myself equally indebted to the Muse that helps me' (*LWC* i, 305).[22] Here the Muse's power is jokingly reduced to the means by which Cowper can acknowledge (and indirectly request) gifts from his friends. His next letter to Hill reveals the result of this hint. Thanking his friend 'for the Idea of a Basket of Fish' (which evidently hasn't arrived), he notes that 'Your Approbation of my last Heliconian Present, encourages me to send you another' (*LWC* i, 308).

Again, the allusion to Mount Helicon (the seat of the Muses) is mock-heroic. Far from making a serious claim on classical inspiration, Cowper's playfulness suggests that the enclosed poem is the result of craft rather than divine intervention. Significantly, the piece in question is 'On the Promotion of

Edward Thurlow Esq To the Lord Chancellorship of England'. Hill and Cowper had known Thurlow when they were law students, and Thurlow had recently given Hill the post of Secretary of Lunatics – Thurlow was therefore, in a sense, Hill's patron.[23] This triangulation between the poet, his patron, and his patron's patron recalls the Cowper-Hesketh-Montagu triangle. In both cases, Cowper's poetry mediates between different levels of affluence; as such, his writing is angled at the needs and/or vanity of the people above him in the chain.

To be effective Cowper's 'Heliconian Present' must acknowledge its own constructedness. By drawing attention to the poem's status as a made object, Cowper shows Hill that the piece has been tailored specifically to his tastes: 'I wrote it indeed on purpose for you, for my Subjects are not always such as I could hope would prove agreeable to You' (*LWC* i, 308). The rewards of this bespoke approach are shown by the letter's postscript which notes that 'The Fish are come since this was written, for which – Thanks...The Herrings are remarkably fine' (*LWC* i, 310). This in turn leads Cowper to emphasize craftsmanship rather than poetic theory, and monetary – rather than aesthetic – value.

Thus Cowper compares himself, in another letter, to a gem smith: 'a Lapidary I suppose accounts it a Laborious part of his Business to Rub away the Roughness of the Stone, but it is my Amusement; & if after all the Polishing I can give it, it discovers some little Lustre, I think myself well rewarded for my Pains'. Significantly, the same missive announces that he is going to set fees for his poetic enclosures.

> I shall charge you a Halfpenny a piece for ev'ry Copy I send you, the Short as well as the long. This is a sort of after clap you little expected, but I cannot possibly afford them at a cheaper Rate. If this Method of raising Money had occurred to me sooner, I should have made the Bargain sooner...It will be a considerable Encouragement to my Muse, and Act as a powerfull Stimulus to my Industry'. (*LWC* i, 402–3)

The tone is tongue-in-cheek. But in a sense Cowper did charge his correspondents, albeit indirectly. Eighteenth-century postal charges were paid by the recipient, not the sender; however MPs were entitled to free postage, and their pre-franked covers were often distributed far beyond their legitimate range. Many of Cowper's correspondences were subsidized by parliamentary franks; his letters note when he is running low, so that his friends can replenish the stock. Sometimes he also used the franks for sending manuscripts to his publishers.[24]

This practice saved his correspondents' money as well as his own; and Cowper was hardly alone in abusing parliamentary privilege. But by the same token, franks were a valuable commodity, and Cowper is careful to discharge the debt through his writing. Or, as he tells one friend, 'As I Promised you Verse if you would send me a Frank, I am not willing to return the Cover without some' (*LWC* i, 376). These franking arrangements remind us that literary discourse is framed by economic exchange – even the letter form, which has often been represented as the least mercantile of genres.

Because letters appear to circulate in private, nostalgic commentators frequently depict eighteenth-century correspondence as the record of a more courtly age than our own.[25] Eighteenth-century letters are certainly governed by writerly etiquette but as Austen's fiction reminds us, manners are also bound up with social regulation and with questions of power, class and status. This is true for Cowper, whose letters and poetry perform a gentlemanly register that is far from secure. Indeed much of their brilliance comes from the tension between his desire to look respectable and his contradictory need to remind the reader that he still needs financial help. Fear of poverty and the urge to stay genteel are therefore not incidental to Cowper's work; nor are they 'merely' biographical. Rather, they power Cowper's writing as much as his life.

These factors also underlie Cowper's use of subscription publishing. On one hand, a successful subscription demonstrated social reach and literary desirability. (Cowper was pleased to have gained almost as many subscribers as Pope did for *his* Homer translation.)[26] However the subscription system could also be seen as a capitalist extension of the bartering that already existed between Cowper and his friends. The main difference is that with subscription publishing, the writer received cash rather than herrings; as a consequence, it was more prestigious. However by the same token, Cowper's subscription was less egalitarian than barter because it both displayed, and depended on, privilege. (Cowper couldn't have made the scheme work without access to Lady Hesketh's social circles, or those of his other agents.) Moreover, not all writers had Cowper's advantages – as I'll show in the next section.

## 'LACTILLA'S VACANT SOUL'

Three years before Cowper wrote about the feather room, Mrs Montagu received a poem from Ann Yearsley, the so-called 'poetical milkwoman of Bristol'. Using another of the bird metaphors that Montagu seems to have attracted, Yearsley depicted the famous bluestocking outstripping man's achievements by taking flight.

> [W]ith firm wing
> Swift she o'ertakes *his* Muse, which spread afar
> Its brightest glories in the days of yore;
> Lo! where she, mounting, spurns the steadfast earth,
> And, sailing on the cloud of science, bears
> The banner of Perfection.

> (*EWP* 395)

Yearsley was more successful than Cowper in catching Montagu's eye. Besides contributing twenty-two guineas, Montagu helped run the subscription list for Yearsley's first volume. Between them, Montagu and Hannah More (who 'discovered' Yearsley) gathered over a thousand subscribers, including 'seven duchesses and sixteen countesses, a number of bishops, as well as Reynolds, Walpole, Burney, the Blue-stockings, and many other prominent names'. This wasn't bad for someone whom More had described as 'a milker of Cows, and a feeder of Hogs, who has never even *seen* a Dictionary' (*EWP* 392–3).

Yearsley's success, and the terms in which More described her working life, typify the late eighteenth-century interest in primitivism. As a provincial working-class woman, Yearsley was represented as a 'natural' genius whose poetical ability outshone her humble context. As such, she was part of a vogue that would later include William Wordsworth's contributions to the *Lyrical Ballads* (1798–1802). The primitivist craze helps explain why Yearsley gained more subscribers than Cowper. Homer translations were high status – but a bit stuffy. However a poetical milkmaid was something new, even if the selling point was the writer's background rather than her poetry.

This last point is important because it shows that 'the primitive' was itself a commodity. But though Yearsley gained more subscribers than Cowper, primitivism was a socially limiting identity. While the 'peasant poets' of this period were often better educated than their advocates admitted,[27] the 'primitive' qualities on which they were sold could act as a barrier to further advancement. Yearsley has become a celebrated instance of this because More and Montagu refused to hand over her subscription money. Instead they advanced her £20 and invested a further £350 (in their names, not hers) so as to give her an annual income of £18. Not wanting to spoil their *protégée* for a life of useful labour, Montagu and More gave her enough money to improve her circumstances but not enough to support a writing career. Instead, More wanted her to run a school.

This typified the experience of eighteenth-century working-class writers. As John Clare would later discover, ongoing success hinged on middle-class taste; and writers often depended on autocratic patrons with paternalistic assumptions. This is where Cowper's gentility comes into its own. Cowper seems to have been disappointed that his subscription didn't raise more money, but at least there was no question of his having to wrestle his £1,000 from Lady Hesketh's grasp. And nor would he have dreamt of turning on Hesketh; for theirs was a comfortable arrangement in which both parties reflected back the image that the other wanted to see.

By contrast, Yearsley had to fight against the circumscribed existence that More and Montagu had designed for her. In doing so she made herself unpopular with her fashionable subscribers, most of whom saw her as an ungrateful upstart. It was a tribute to her tenacity, as well as her talent, that she eventually gained a different patron, reclaimed the capital from her subscription volume, published further volumes of poetry, had a play performed, and wrote a novel that is said to have earned her £200. Before getting to that point, though, she had to face down More's attempt to control her output and income. When direct appeals came to nothing, she denounced More in print and threatened to petition the king. In response, Montagu noted that Yearsley's dead child 'might have risen to some great station – in botany bay'[28] while More called her 'a savage' with a 'reprobate mind' (*EWP* 393).

The route from 'primitive' genius to 'savage' was evidently a short one for working-class writers who refused to observe the protocols of patronage. By breaking these rules, Yearsley exposed her work – as well as her life – to More's accusations. Hitting where it hurt, More claimed that she had had to re-write the poems to make them scan; Yearsley retaliated by saying that More had tried to ruin her work out of jealousy. Yearsley's later volumes suggest that there was no truth to More's accusation, but the terms of the dispute reveal the extent to which literary patronage was (and is) about control as much as liberation. Patronage could be enabling, but only within certain parameters. Speaking out of turn was not encouraged.

Given this, it's fascinating that Yearsley later opened a circulating library. What better image can there be of her escape from More's control? Not only did she invest her capital in ways that she herself chose, she used the capital to make writing available to other people. (As well as to earn herself more money.) By doing so she exerted command over the same discourses that More had used against her: she was now a purveyor of texts with the power to shape other people's tastes. And though commentators are divided over the library's success, Yearsley was evidently a canny operator. Her poem to Montagu (which I cited at the beginning of this section) claims that the bluestocking struck awe into 'Lactilla's vacant soul'. However subsequent events demonstrated that 'Lactilla' (i.e. Yearsley) was neither so 'vacant' nor so awestruck as to accept Montagu's and More's manipulations. On the contrary, Yearsley's initial supplications begin to look like a studied pose.

Consider, too, the name 'Lactilla'. Designed to resemble the Cynthias and Amaryllises of pastoral poetry, Lactilla is an invention based on the Latin for milk ('lacte'). On one level, the name reminded Yearsley's audience of her occupation. However 'Lactilla' also suggests a clever fusion of classical and primitivist references. It was a way of saying that here, at last, was a genuinely pastoral writer – someone whose livelihood actually depended on pastures. (By comparison, one can't imagine Thomas Gray tending sheep or milking cattle.) And although these terms were ultimately limiting, Yearsley's use of them can be seen (for better or worse) as an experiment in branding. Significantly, her last volume was called *The Rural Lyre* (1796).

I want to close by returning to Cowper because he too was using a brand: that of gentleman poet. In discussing the patronage networks that surrounded Cowper and Montagu, I don't mean to imply that Cowper should be condemned for being middle-class. After all, he had no more control over his birth than Yearsley had over hers. However I do think that Cowper's investment in his own gentility produces a world-view that impacts on other people as much as on himself. For example, *The Task* describes the labourer who does heavy work in the poet's garden as 'bred to toil' (*PWC* ii, 173). Similarly, an illiterate waggoner is 'form'd to bear' the appalling weather that surrounds him (*PWC* ii, 195).

The eighteenth century saw decisive breakthroughs in the development of modern plant and animal strains, and Cowper was a keen reader of gardening manuals: he had a sophisticated awareness of artificial propagation, cross-pollination, and inter-breeding. In this context, the phrases 'bred to toil' and 'form'd to bear' are far from neutral. Rather, they reveal a casual assumption that the working-classes are oblivious to emotional refinement because they have been prepared for their labours by generations of similarly unrefined forefathers. It's not that Cowper is a eugenicist in the modern sense. It's more that he doesn't even have to be a eugenicist because his class politics take it for granted that people will and should be kept within their existing castes. Or, as he puts it in *The Task*:

> Man in society is like a flow'r
> Blown in its native bed. 'Tis there alone
> His properties expanded in full bloom
> Shine out, there only reach their proper use.

> (*PWC* ii, 203)

The 'native bed' is the one to which we are born; if we leave it we will rot. And note the phrase 'their proper use'. Labourers will have one 'use', we assume, while gentleman-poets will have another.

A final literary anecdote.

The year before be wrote 'On Mrs Montagu's Feather-Hangings', Cowper read Robert Burns's first book of poetry.

Impressed, he wrote that Burns was the first writer from 'the lower rank of life' since Shakespeare or Matthew Prior 'who need not be indebted for any part of his praise, to a charitable consideration of his origin, and the disadvantages under which he has laboured'. However Cowper added that 'It will be a pity if he should not hereafter divest himself of barbarism, and content himself with writing pure English, in which he appears perfectly qualified to excel' (*LWC* iii, 16).

The year after, Cowper advised Lady Hesketh that 'I [do not] think him worth your purchasing' because although he was 'an extraordinary Genius his measure and his language are so terribly barbarous, that he is not a pleasing poet to an English reader' (*LWC* iii, 145). Hesketh evidently read the poems anyway because Cowper's next letter shows him agreeing with her choice of favourite pieces. However he added, damningly, that

> Could a Nightingale be so unhappy as to acquire the scream of a Jay, she would furnish an instance somewhat resembling the case of a good poet writing in a detestable language. A man may whistle well, but if his breath be offensive one would [not w]ish to sit within the wind of him. Poor Burns [is eve]r in this predicament. (*LWC* iii, 168)

Burns, though, would have the last laugh. Despite his wayward refusal to make himself accessible to middle-class English readers, he remains a best-seller – with or without the bad breath. Cowper cannot boast as much. And as for Montagu's feather-hangings – they fell prey to moths and changing tastes. And though her mansion lasted longer it, too, has gone. Bombed in the Blitz, it was finally demolished in 1945.

# 3

# The Occasions of Poetry

Thom Gunn argues, in a 1985 essay, that Ben Jonson's poetry has been neglected because

> so much of it can be damned as 'occasional'. That is, much of it is elicited by external events, or is intended to compliment some noble, or is written to commend another person's book. And nowadays we tend to use the phrase 'occasional poetry' to indicate trivial or insincere writing.[1]

Ben Jonson lies outside the scope of this book – he died in 1637. Occasional poetry, however, is central to eighteenth-century poetic practice. Most of the poems from the previous chapter fall into this category, and the British Library catalogue features over one hundred eighteenth-century books with variations of the title 'Poems on Several Occasions'. This includes work by such influential writers as John Gay, Matthew Prior, and Christopher Smart. Moreover several seventeenth- and eighteenth-century editions describe Shakespeare's sonnets as 'occasional' works. However, the number of new volumes with this title falls dramatically in the nineteenth and twentieth centuries.

This chapter will argue, not just for the validity of occasional writing, but also for its importance to ongoing poetic traditions. First, I will try to define occasional poetry. (This is not as easy as it sounds.) I will then ask why occasional poetry remains undertheorized and undervalued. This will involve relating occasional poetry to another eighteenth-century discourse, the sublime, as well as to insights from postmodernism, New Criticism and Marxist literary criticism. A recurring preoccupation will be the tension between materialist and immanent approaches to occasional poetry; the tension, that is, between readings that place poems inside or outside an historical trajectory. In particular, I mean to extend the insights of the previous chapter

44

by using pre-romantic occasional poetry as a defamiliarizing device through which we might become newly aware of how romantic ideologies dominate current attitudes to poetry, culture and identity.[2] I want to begin, though, by asking what occasional poetry actually is, and why its status is unstable.

## DEFINING OCCASIONAL POETRY

Irrespective of the object of analysis, generic definitions usually oscillate between an impulse to universalize and an impulse to minoritize. That is, we define genres either by making everything fit into them, or by allowing only a few, rigidly-described works to make the grade. Picking the first of these routes, Thom Gunn writes that 'all poetry is occasional: whether the occasion is an external event like a birthday or a declaration of war, whether it is an occasion of the imagination, or whether it is...some sort of combination of the two'.[3] By contrast, John Dolan argues that occasional poetry 'relies on a verifiable event as its genesis' and that 'occasional poems are not in any simple sense meant to be taken as works of the imagination'. Moreover occasional poetry 'tends to be funereal poetry': that is, it marks the passing of public and private figures.[4] Irreconcilable though these accounts may seem, they can be connected via Dolan's argument that eighteenth-century writers struggled to expand earlier concepts of occasional poetry until the form could include internal as well as external occurrences. Gunn's permissive definition is therefore made possible by the changes that Dolan traces in eighteenth-century writing – changes that culminate (for Dolan) in the work of William Wordsworth.

Although Dolan and Gunn envision different kinds of trigger, they agree that occasional poetry draws attention to a specific moment, whether public or private. A working definition of occasional poetry might therefore be that it springs from, commemorates, or helps to create, a happening. But, as Gunn acknowledges, 'occasional poetry' also tends to mean 'trivial or insincere writing'. We therefore need to ask why some works are given this label while others are not. An astonishingly large number of romantic poems announce, by their titles, that they are occasional, yet readers bring different assumptions to John

45

Keats's 'On First Looking into Chapman's Homer' (1816) than they do to William Cowper's 'To the Immortal Memory of the Halybutt, on which I dined this Day, Monday, April 26, 1784'. This imbalance suggests that approaches to occasional poetry are dogged by value judgements even more than by uncertainty as to what constitutes an 'occasion'; it also suggests that certain kinds of occasion may be granted more status than others.

The negativity with which 'the occasional' is viewed from the late eighteenth-century onwards can be inferred from the Oxford English Dictionary. When applied to 'a speech, literary composition, [or] religious service', the OED defines 'occasional' as that which is 'produced on, or intended for, a special occasion. Hence occasional speaker, writer, etc., one who delivers occasional speeches or writes occasional verses, pamphlets, etc'. The OED's first illustration of this meaning comes from 1687; the quotation refers to St Paul's letters and doesn't involve aesthetic judgements. (The OED lifts this example from Samuel Johnson's *A Dictionary of the English Language* (1755); the original source is John Dryden's *The Hind and the Panther*.) The next OED citation is a matter-of-fact reference, from 1701, to 'Letters [and] Occasional Speeches'. However in 1779–81, L. P. Johnson remarks that 'no height of excellence can be expected' from 'an occasional performance'. The *Manchester Guardian* delivers a comparable verdict a century later, noting that 'verses [that] are purely occasional' have 'no claim to stability' – that is, they cannot make an ongoing call on readerly attention.

Eighteenth- and nineteenth-century dictionaries provide further examples of how 'occasional poetry' moves from neutrally descriptive uses to ones that encode certain values or assumptions. Even so, positive uses persist, albeit residually: the OED cites Samuel Hynes calling W. B. Yeats's 'Easter 1916' an 'occasional' poem – the occasion being the Irish Revolutionary Brotherhood's failed attempt to institute an independent Irish state by seizing control of central Dublin. Here we seem to be a long way from Cowper's poem on Elizabeth Montagu's feather room. Not only is the magnitude of the occasion different, so too is the perceived quality of both the poet and the poem. I will return to the emotional scale of 'the occasion' in the final third of this chapter, but for now I just want to note that the OED's citations show the difficulty of defining a genre through examples.

Nor does definition become easier if we limit our selections to a particular period. Eighteenth-century instances of occasional poetry might include Elizabeth Thomas's 'On Sir J. S. saying in a Sarcastic Manner, My Books would make me Mad. An Ode' (1722), Samuel Wesley's 'On the Setting up of Mr Butler's Monument in Westminster Abbey' (1726), Mary Barber's 'On Seeing an Officer's Widow distracted, who had been driven to Despair by a long and fruitless Solicitation for the Arrears of her Pension' (1734), Thomas Gray's 'Ode on the Death of a Favourite Cat, Drowned in a Tub of Gold Fishes' (1748), William Collin's 'Ode Occasioned by the Death of Mr Thomson' (1749), Mary Leapor's 'Upon her Play being returned to her, stained with Claret' (1751), Thomas Warton's 'Verses on Sir Joshua Reynolds's Painted Window at New College, Oxford' (1782), and Robert Burns's 'To a Louse, On Seeing one on a Lady's Bonnet at Church' (1786). As well as producing an unwieldy list, this approach uncovers texts that prove to be surprisingly disparate – as their titles indicate.

Of course the clumsiness of such lists is precisely why it is hard to write generic definitions that are both consistent and inclusive. But although generic categorizations create as many problems as they solve, keeping them in play allows us to ask why some equally problematic labels, such as 'the Gothic', have been granted more credibility than 'the occasional'. Until relatively recently, novels such as Horace Walpole's *The Castle of Otranto* (1764) and Matthew Lewis's *The Monk* (1796) were seen, at best, as marginal to the canon, yet Gothic fiction now enjoys a currency that occasional poetry seems unlikely to achieve. This is partly because the Gothic novel can be re-described as popular culture whereas occasional poetry is assumed to be elitist. Arguably, however, occasional poetry is less elitist than the Gothic: the former often concerns everyday domesticity whereas Gothicism focuses, by its nature, on feudal social structures.[5] In any case, although the Gothic is defined in contradictory ways, few of the definitions are burdened with the implications of worthlessness that crowd around poems like Gray's 'Ode on the Death of a Favourite Cat, Drowned in a Tub of Gold Fishes' (which Samuel Johnson famously described as 'a trifle, but...not a happy trifle').[6]

This helps explain the shiftiness with which even Vincent

Newey – a staunch advocate of mid eighteenth-century poetry – deals with occasional writing. Newey may well be right that 'some of Cowper's "comic" and "occasional" poems are coloured by the darker side of his interior life',[7] but his scare-quotes suggest that if comic and/or occasional poems are ... to be taken seriously they need ballast from 'darker' aspects of life. Pursuing his point, Newey writes that Cowper's 'Epitaph on a Hare' contains 'something more than good nature, or humanity, or drollery' and that 'the emotional life of the poem has its heavier side'.[8] Meanwhile 'On the Death of Mrs Throckmorton's Bulfinch' offers a 'mirror-image' of the poet's 'foreseen destruction' by a Calvinist God, while 'On a Goldfinch Starved to Death in his Cage' is 'almost Blakeian'.[9]

Using David Gascoyne's 1930s poem 'The Very Image' as illustration, Newey argues that Cowper's elegies for dead animals 'could be described in some respects as proto-*surrealist* poems'.[10] This suggests that a relatively modern discourse – such as surrealism – must be applied to Cowper's work before it can be redeemed for a contemporary audience. In a similar move, Conrad Brunström wonders if 'one means of finally rescuing Cowper from the label "protoromantic" is ... to play-fully label him a "protopostmodern"'. To be fair, Brunström adds that such a label is 'too bizarre ... ever to cohere (let alone calcify) into any kind of critical orthodoxy': he is not so much classifying Cowper as exploring how his work might look through a different lens.[11] Even so, it's striking that both he and Newey try to validate Cowper by nudging the poet forward on the literary-historical scale.

In theory, such moves could unsettle literary history in the manner I suggested in Chapter 1, but for that to happen there would have to be a scepticism about literary discourse, as well as about historical linearity. (That is, there would need to be a recognition that literature is a discourse and not a transcendent, god-given form.) However by recommending surrealist and post-modernist frameworks, these commentators seem to advance Cowper's standing by buying uncritically into post-Romantic literary formations. Moreover, Brunström undermines his own advocacy by writing that Cowper is 'undoubtedly' a 'lesser poet than Wordsworth'.[12] By fitting Cowper back into the received literary-historical league table, Brunström allows the ideological category of 'literature' to displace a fuller consideration of Cowper's cultural significance.

Indeed 'cultural significance' is one of the major planks in my defence of the occasional. Literary forms do not appear out of thin air: they speak to, and help to shape, the cultures that produce them. To discount occasional poetry is therefore to fail to ask what work the genre performed in the eighteenth-century imagination. On a more immediate level, it is also to ignore poetry's right to discuss local, topical or everyday issues. Besides the pieces I've already mentioned, Cowper's subjects include a miniature of his mother, the madness of George III, the exhumation of what was thought to be Milton's skeleton, Admiral Rodney's relief of Gibraltar in 1780, the American War of Independence, the Gordon Riots, and the price of tobacco. As well as illuminating eighteenth-century life, these poems constitute an argument for what one might call a poetics of materiality – by which I mean a form of poetry that reflects upon objects and their relation to history.

Considering scholarship's current interest in 'pots and pans, needles and pins... *material objects stuff'*, Alan Sinfield warns against 'a kind of textual anthropology' in which good work may be done but where 'the political edge is blunted'.[13] With this in mind, I mean to look at objects, not for their own sake, but for what they tell us about the power structures of the societies in which they circulate. I pursued a version of this approach in the last chapter when I explored the cultural significance of Elizabeth Montagu's feather room. I now want to consider two ways of conceptualizing the materiality of occasional poetry: New Criticism and Marxism. As well as producing a fuller understanding of the critical contexts in which we read occasional poetry, this comparison will lead into my subsequent analysis of the relationship between the occasional and the sublime.

## ICONS AND URNS

Thomas Gray's 'Ode on the Death of a Favourite Cat, Drowned in a Tub of Gold Fishes' (1747) is a good place to think about occasional poetry's place in the material world. As the tone of its

49

title suggests, the poem is a mock-heroic elegy in which the heroine ('pensive Selima') is a cat who loses her life (rather than her virginity) when she ill-advisedly pursues her owner's carp.

As usual with mock heroic writing, the poem's humour comes from the gap between an elevated style and a mundane subject. Thus, the water in the tub is a 'lake', the cat is a 'hapless nymph', and the fish are the 'genii of the stream'. In one detail, though, Gray's language is not overly inflated. We know that the 'tub' of the title was indeed a 'lofty vase' inscribed with 'China's gayest art' because it belonged – like Selima herself – to Gray's friend, Horace Walpole, who was a noted collector of *objets d'art* (*GCG* 78–85). Moreover, the tub can still be viewed in Walpole's home, Strawberry Hill, and it is the subject of a John Carter watercolour that shows the basin displayed on a pedestal in Walpole's Little Cloister.

This pedestal – which also survives – was commissioned by Walpole in 1773, two years after Gray's death. In a turn that neatly underlines the poem's interest in material objects, Walpole ordered that the pedestal be inscribed with the first stanza of Gray's 'Ode'. Thus the poem itself becomes an object – a material, as well as a linguistic, text. This effect is augmented by Carter's portrayal of the vase on its pedestal, and by subsequent reproductions of Carter's painting. Cumulatively, these objectifications turn the poem, literally, into a verbal icon. Here, of course, I am echoing a phrase popularized by W. K. Wimsatt who was, with Cleanth Brooks, the most influential of the New Critics who flourished in 1940s and 1950s America. Wimsatt's best-known book, *The Verbal Icon*, holds that a successful poem 'takes on something like the character of a stone statue or a porcelain vase. Through its meaning or meanings the poem is. It has an iconic solidity'.[14] Wimsatt's image echoes Cleanth Brooks's *The Well Wrought Urn* (1947), which argues that poetry should be apprehended as a self-sufficient linguistic structure. Brooks's title comes from John Donne's 'The Canonization' (published 1633), and his book contains classic readings of poems such as Gray's 'Elegy Written in a Country Churchyard' (1751) and Keats's 'Ode on a Grecian Urn' (1820). These examples show Brooks's predilection for poems featuring objects, particularly ones that combine aesthetic appeal with a sacramental function. Such texts reinforce

Brooks's notion that poetry is itself an artefact; and not just any artefact, either, but one with a ritual significance – for Keats's urn, like Donne's, is a funeral vessel.

Given this, it's striking that Brooks discusses Gray's 'Elegy' rather the 'Ode on the Death of a Favourite Cat, Drowned in a Tub of Gold Fishes'. It's true that Gray's 'Elegy' refers, in passing, to a 'storied urn' containing the 'silent dust' of the dead (*GCG* 125), but the 'Ode' on the cat is much more directly focused on the china vase mentioned in its title. Walpole's 'tub', moreover, is the means by which 'pensive Selima' meets her unfortunate end; therefore it, too, is a mortuary container. These circumstances ought to make the 'Ode on the Death of a Favourite Cat' perfect for Brooks. However his failure even to mention the poem suggests that comic works don't really fit his agenda, especially when they mock the content and imagery of more 'serious' pieces: a 'tub' is not the same as an urn. Perhaps Brooks also favours the 'storied urn' of the 'Elegy Written in a Country Churchyard' because the phrase is non-specific. The urn is 'storied' in the sense that it carries a visual narrative, but the poem reveals nothing about the provenance of the urn or its decoration. The same is true of Keats's Grecian urn: even if Keats had a single vase in mind (which he almost certainly hadn't) we have no way of knowing whose ashes it contained or the hands through which it passed before Keats saw it. As a consequence, both vessels can easily be turned into metaphors. By contrast, the 'tub' in Gray's 'Ode on the Death of a Favourite Cat' is highly particular. We know what it looks like because it was displayed on Walpole's plinth and is reproduced through Carter's painting.

In addition, the vase is implicated in a traceable pattern of exchange. As part of the flourishing trade in eastern objects, Walpole's urn can be placed alongside Elizabeth Montagu's feather room as an instance of how imported goods are used to produce 'exotic' décor effects. Moreover, the vase's later history shows that literary and cultural celebrity was itself becoming commodifiable. When it was sold at auction in 1842, the piece was described as 'the celebrated large blue and white oriental china cistern, on a Gothic carved pedestal, in which Horace Walpole's cat was drowned; this gave occasion to Mr Gray, the poet, to write his beautiful ode' (*GCG* 79). (The Earl of Derby bought it for forty guineas.) Given the vase's economic worth, it's appropriate that Gray's poem is also linked to money – this time through patronage. In one of literary history's most mysterious fallings out, Gray and Walpole had quarrelled in 1741 while doing the Grand Tour; they returned separately to England and their friendship lapsed for four years. The 'Ode on the Death of a Favourite Cat' was written just over a year after their reconciliation, and the poem is a token of the renewed friendship. However it can also be taken as an attempt, on Gray's part, to exert a poetic identity that might offset Walpole's social and financial muscle. Their Grand Tour row seems to have been due, at least in part, to Gray's resentment of Walpole's condescension: since Walpole was bankrolling the trip, he felt entitled to follow his own desires rather than those of his much poorer companion. By poking fun at Walpole's expensive furnishings the 'Ode' acknowledges the friends' economic disparity while simultaneously declaring Gray's alternative power source as poet and sometime satirist.

The financial exchanges that surround Gray's ode present a different kind of iconic solidity to the one offered by Wimsatt and Brooks, and not only because the urns, vases and icons towards which the New Critics gravitate are metaphorical, not literal. By arguing that we should examine poetry in the light of eternity ('*sub specie aeternitatis*')[15] rather than via its historical context, Brooks construes poems as unchanging art objects, rather than as products to be bought and sold. By contrast I favour an economically informed analysis in which art objects are revealed as commodities. For example, note how the Strawberry Hill sales catalogue links Walpole's vase to the occasionality of Gray's poem: 'the celebrated large blue and white oriental china cistern...in which Horace Walpole's cat was drowned; this gave occasion to Mr Gray...to write his beautiful ode'. According to this logic, the poem is 'occasioned' by a luxury item, and the luxury item gains further value from the poem. By foregrounding objects as objects (rather than as metaphors), this approach promotes insights that are forbidden by the ahistorical formalism of Brooks and Wimsatt; this line of enquiry also suggests that eighteenth-century occasional poetry is peculiarly suited to materialist readings.

Crucially for my purposes, the materiality of eighteenth-century occasional poetry hints at the material and occasional aspects that are often suppressed in discussions of later, romantic period writing. (This is an example of how pre-romantic poetry can defamiliarize romantic ideology.) For instance, Keats's 'Ode on a Grecian Urn' is open to the same sorts of analysis that I have applied to Gray's 'Ode on the Death of a Favourite Cat, Drowned in a Tub of Gold Fishes'; this is even more true of Keats's poems on the recently transported Elgin marbles. In a less obvious vein, poems of literary tourism such as Keats's 'On Seeing a Lock of Milton's Hair. Ode', 'Lines on the Mermaid Tavern' and 'Lines Written in the Highlands after a Visit to Burns's Country' (all 1818) reveal the nineteenth-century roots of what later becomes the heritage industry. (Note, too, Wordsworth's 'Address to the Sons of Burns, after visiting their father's grave, August 14th, 1803'.)

This line of analysis also prompts a re-evaluation of poems that seem to present a more fully transcendent version of literary culture, especially the pieces in which Keats reflects on the reading experience, such as 'On First Looking into Chapman's Homer' (1816), 'Written on a Blank Space at the End of Chaucer's Tale of *The Floure and the Leafe*' (1817), 'On Sitting Down to Read *King Lear* Once Again' (1818), and 'A Dream, after reading Dante's Episode of Paolo and Francesca' (1819). The objects in these texts are less easily reducible to their physical dimensions: as books they mobilize fantasies that go beyond the pages in the reader's hands. Even so, academia's recent turn towards histories of the book has exposed the materiality that underlies the reading experience.[16] Moreover, Keats's metaphors for reading are themselves replete with political implications. To choose an obvious example, 'On First Looking into Chapman's Homer' represents reading as a quasi-imperial activity: opening the *Iliad* makes Keats feel as if he's conquering Central America.[17]

These poems suggest that romantic poetry often offers a rhetoric of escape that is in tension with material histories that may or may not be acknowledged by either the writer or the reader. Interestingly, there are comparable tensions in New Criticism's attempt to separate poetry from history. In Wimsatt's case, removing poetry from history means that literary form becomes a kind of sacrament, hence the religious connotations of the term 'icon'. The quasi-religious authority of the 'verbal icon' protects Wimsatt's favoured poems from critics who want to look 'beyond' the poem to the contexts in which literature is written and read. Wimsatt, though, is quite happy to look 'beyond' the poem to religion. (His chapter on 'Poetry and Morals' remarks that 'the greatest poetry will be morally right'.)[18] But although the language is different, Wimsatt's moral imperatives are oddly close to the absolutes of romantic ideology, not least because both discourses attach transcendent possibilities to literary texts. This will become clearer in the next section, where I discuss the plenitude and excess of the romantic sublime. For now I just want to note that neither New Criticism nor High Romanticism do justice to occasional poetry, especially if the poem in question features an object that blocks its own transfiguration. That's why Keats's 'Ode on a Grecian Urn' is more canonical than Mary Jones's 'Soliloquy on an Empty Purse' (1750). It's also why the first of these poems fits the patterns proposed by Brooks and Wimsatt while other Keats texts, such as 'To Mrs Reynolds's Cat' (1818), do not.

I have discussed New Criticism at length because it offers an apparently attractive, but actually hazardous, approach to occasional poetry. Objects are central to New Critical imagery but Brooks and Wimsatt are selective about both the objects and the poems that they endorse. In particular, New Criticism celebrates poems that can be presented as self-sustaining artefacts. But what about objects and texts with a more open form?[19] How do they relate to occasional poetry? Can the urn be cracked or incomplete, and what would this mean for our understanding of occasional poetry? To answer these questions, I want to explore a formation that enjoys more currency than New Criticism, and that tends to place the 'open' over the 'closed'. The discourse in question – the sublime – is both paradigmatically romantic and highly-prized by postmodern theory. As such, it provides an invaluable place to explore both the historical and the continuing marginalization of occasional poetry. A particular strand of the argument will be that New Criticism's attraction to the closed and the self-sufficient is echoed, paradoxically, by postmodernism's attraction to the unbounded – with neither offering much support to pre-romantic instances of occasional poetry.

## SUBLIMITY, ROMANTICISM AND FORM

Jean-François Lyotard's classic essay, 'The Sublime and the Avant-Garde' (1984) argues that the sublime 'is perhaps the only mode of artistic sensibility to characterize the modern'. Linking sublimity to eighteenth-century Europe's exploration of the 'contradictory feeling' of 'joy and anxiety, exaltation and depression', Lyotard writes that in the late eighteenth century, the sublime ousted classical poetics with the result that 'romanticism, in other words, modernity, triumphed'.[20] In another essay, 'What is Postmodernism?', Lyotard invokes sublimity as the originator of both modernism and postmodernism.[21]

By identifying romanticism with (post)modernity, Lyotard implies that pre-romantic poetry (which he does not discuss) falls short of articulating what it means to be alive in the 'modern' moment. This is hardly new: Chapter 1 discussed similar attitudes. But Lyotard's emphasis on sublimity as the defining characteristic of both romanticism and modernity is illuminating, not least because many mid-eighteenth-century poems seem to evade, or actively reject, sublime gestures. In particular, eighteenth-century occasional poems rarely manifest the radical uncertainty that Lyotard associates with sublimity; indeed this is one of the main reasons that they continue to be neglected. And although it would be unreasonable to expect eighteenth-century poetry to follow a template set by postmodern theory, we should remember that Lyotard doesn't initiate the link between sublimity and indeterminacy. On the contrary, when Lyotard writes that 'the aesthetics of the sublime' are 'more indeterminate' than those of the beautiful, and that 'pleasure mixed with pain' produces the 'extreme tension...that characterizes the pathos of the sublime',[22] he is following two of the eighteenth century's most influential theorists, Edmund Burke and Immanuel Kant. Although their approaches differ, Burke and Kant help create the aesthetic standards that inform romantic period criticism. Their influence is also detectable in the shape and content of much romantic literature. If we explore how the indeterminacy of the sublime is represented and theorized in late-eighteenth and early-nineteenth-century culture, we can then see how these sublime forms rebound on our readings of earlier eighteenth-century poetry.

Towards the end of the century, Kant writes in his *Critique of Judgement* (1790) that the beautiful, in nature, 'consists in [the object's] being bounded' whereas the sublime can be 'found in a formless object' because the latter activates an 'unboundedness' that prompts the viewer to imagine the 'totality' that the object itself fails to present.[23] Sublimity therefore produces an irresolvable oscillation between the sight of an unbounded object (such as a mountain, the top of which is shrouded in cloud) and the viewer's attempt to impose closure onto that object (by imagining what the top might look like). The result is a mental opposition in which neither image can win: instead each is held in dynamic tension with the other. This interest in indeterminacy is in many ways a logical development of mid-eighteenth-century taste, hence the period's preoccupation with the fractured and the incomplete.[24] Real and artificial ruins had been fashionable aspects of garden designs from the mid-eighteenth century onwards and there are textual fissures in some of the best known fictions of the time, including Samuel Richardson's *Pamela* (1740–01) and Laurence Sterne's *Tristram Shandy* (1759–67). Novels of sensibility, such as Henry Mackenzie's *The Man of Feeling* (1771), frequently feature narrative breaks attributed to gaps in 'actual' manuscript sources.

In poetry, the same trends are exemplified by the pseudo-medieval Ossian and Rowley poems of James Macpherson and Thomas Chatterton. As its title suggests, Macpherson's *Fragments of Ancient Poetry, Collected in the Highlands of Scotland* (1760) uses textual interruption to substantiate a claim on archaic status: the fragment is a marker of (alleged) antiquity. Macpherson's Ossian is a sort of Scots Homer, whose sightlessness reminds the reader of the imagination's role in embodying poetic language: just as Ossian has to imagine the scenes he is writing about, so too must the reader use Macpherson's sketch-like text as a trigger for more fully realized mental pictures. In 1768, less than a decade after the first of the Ossian poems were published, Thomas Chatterton claimed that he had discovered a manuscript by Thomas Rowley, a hitherto unknown fifteenth-century poet-cleric. Needless to say, Chatterton had forged the collection himself, but he was not around to enjoy the success of his *Poems* when they were published in 1777. Frustrated by poverty and lack of recognition, he had killed himself seven years before at the age of 17. In doing so, he turned his life into a biographical fragment that would soon be subject to mythic projections. The 'marvellous Boy',[25] as Wordsworth called him, was celebrated by Coleridge and Keats, amongst many others, and his premature end produced a romantic archetype into which Keats and Shelley would themselves be fitted.

Macpherson, Chatterton and their followers helped make fragmentation one of the key devices of romantic period poetry. Coleridge's 'Kubla Khan' (written 1797) is almost as famous for the person from Porlock who interrupts its composition as it is for the sumptuous register in which it is written. Coleridge began 'Christabel' in the same year as 'Kubla Khan' but the tale was still unfinished when he published it in 1816. Wordsworth's *The Prelude* (written 1798–1839, published 1850) was originally intended as the introduction to an even longer poem, *The Recluse*, but the latter was never finished and *The Prelude* exists in multiple forms, none of which can claim to be definitive. Meanwhile, Keats's *Hyperion* (written 1818–9) is subtitled 'A Fragment' as is Coleridge's 'Melancholy' (1797). In addition, fragments are thematically prominent in the romantic period: think of Keats's 'On Seeing the Elgin Marbles' or Percy Bysshe Shelley's 'Ozymandias' (both 1817).

These examples demonstrate a continuity between mid-eighteenth and early nineteenth-century uses of the fragment. At the same time, however, poetic fragmentation throws occasional poetry into striking relief. Although occasional poems sometimes take fragments as their subject, occasional poetry is itself rarely fragmented.[26] Indeed much mid-eighteenth-century occasional poetry would be undone if it adopted a fragmentary form. The Ann Yearsley and William Cowper poems that I discussed in the previous chapter would look different if they were fragments. More important, though, they would also lose their practical effectiveness as tributes to a patron. Elizabeth Montagu, one imagines, would not be a person to accept a broken-off phrase, however potent that unfinished gesture might seem to other eyes.

With this we begin to see why occasional poetry has been subject to such critical disapproval. The rise of the sublime, and the associated importance of the fragment, creates an environment that's inhospitable to the form and diction of much eighteenth-century occasional poetry. The further suspicion that such poetry is written to 'compliment some noble, or...commend another person's book'[27] means that these unfashionable effects become linked to venal motives. Consequently, the tonal effects associated with occasional poetry have become tainted by functional implications. The accusation against these works wouldn't have to be that they are commercially motivated, it could simply be that their language is over instrumental. (Trapped, that is, within literalistic representations of a concrete world.) This would cover poems for patrons, but it could also include decidedly unfiscal poetry, such as Priscilla Pointon's 'Address to a Bachelor on a Delicate Occasion' (1770) – a withering account of how a group of gallants humiliated the blind Pointon by refusing to call a maid to conduct her to the lavatory. One of the men offers to fetch a basin so that she can urinate in front of them, but 'Trueworth' eventually guides her out of the room himself, commenting that 'Your loss [i.e. her disability] the freedom will excuse' (*EWP* 274–5).

Pointon's poem may have seemed less surprising to an eighteenth-century audience than to a modern one. (Her 'Address' is mild compared to some of Jonathan Swift's scatological poems.) But our own surprise underlines the degree to which bodily functions no longer seem appropriate subjects for poetry. Or if they do appear, it's in a spirit of conscious iconoclasm: compare the 'steaming yam' of J. D. McClatchy's 'Feces' (2002)[28] with Priscilla Pointon's matter-of-fact observation that 'Tea, wine and punch, Sir, to be free, / Excellent diuretics be'. Here, as elsewhere, Pointon's rhyme creates a sense of inevitability, hence the poem's decisive finish: 'I repent not what I've done: / Adieu – enjoy your empty fun'. Pointon uses these unambiguous rhymes to underline the speaker's dismissal of the 'Bachelor' who has ill-treated her. Insofar as the poem's most obvious purpose is to give its male addressee a lesson in manners, more tentative rhymes would undermine Pointon's didacticism. As a consequence, the text has very little of the indeterminacy that's associated with the sublime. Significantly, another of Pointon's poems, 'To the Critics' (1794), differentiates her blindness from Homer's and Milton's, insisting that 'I'm not sublimed, / My thoughts are rude, my numbers unrefined' (*EWP* 273-4). The implication is that she, as a woman, inhabits a less exalted sphere than her famous predecessors, both of whom were celebrated by romantic period writers for their 'sublime' effects.

The connection that I'm drawing between the (non-fragmented, non-sublime) form of eighteenth-century occasional poetry and its materialist contents is strengthened if we look at post-romantic attitudes to the rhyming couplets that Pointon and countless of her contemporaries used in poem after poem. In 1880 Matthew Arnold, the most influential critic of the Victorian period, ratified post-romantic anxiety about eighteenth-century verse forms by arguing that Alexander Pope is a '[master] of the art of versification' but lacks 'high seriousness... poetic largeness, freedom, insight'. As a result, Pope belongs among the 'classics of our prose' not the 'classics of our poetry'.[29] Here, Arnold equates 'verse' with prose in order to deny certain writers the 'high seriousness' that he associates with poetry. As well as marginalizing an entire body of writing, Arnold's commentary established what has now become an accepted dichotomy between 'poetry' and 'verse', with the latter marked as subordinate.

Arnold doesn't say much about the 'versification' of which Pope is a master but he presumably means that Pope's rhyming couplets work against the 'largeness' and 'freedom' that he looks for in 'poetry'. Here, though, Arnold is simply following the cue of the early romantics. Coleridge's *Biographia Literaria* (1817) maintains that Pope's writing consists of 'acute observations of men and manners in an artificial state of society' in which 'the logic of wit [is] conveyed in smooth and strong epigrammatic couplets'. Consequently, his work is 'characterized not so much by poetic thoughts, as by *thoughts* translated into the language of poetry'.[30] Meanwhile Wordsworth writes that Pope was 'seduced by an over-love of immediate popularity'; instead of observing nature, he 'dazzled [the nation] by his polished style, and was himself blinded by his own success'.[31]

These comments show how structural devices – such as rhyming couplets – can be made to carry far-reaching associations. They also illustrate how cultural preferences can be presented as self-evident truths. Coleridge's reflections on the 'logic' of Pope's 'smooth' style become reified in Arnold's less tentative view of Pope as a 'versifier' whose work is more like prose than poetry. And note the unexamined assumption, first in Coleridge and then in Arnold, that poetry has an essence that evades logical capture. Pope is found wanting because he thinks in prose; his thoughts can't be re-cast as poetry because poetry (for Coleridge) is a form in which language and thought are indissolubly fused at the moment of speech. It is notoriously difficult to translate poetry into a foreign language because metre and rhythm depend on precise patterns that don't always carry into other tongues, but Coleridge isn't talking about the relationship between different languages. Rather, he's talking about the relationship, in any given language, between words and thoughts. He presents poetry as aspiring to the condition that language enjoyed before the Fall, when God created the world by naming its constituent parts, and where there was no division between objects and their names. Adam inherits this naming privilege (and the authority it conveys) until he and Eve become sinners – thereafter the signifier/signified relationship breaks down.[32] True poetry goes some way to rectifying this linguistic decay, but Pope is stuck in a lower form of utterance which covers its inadequacy with a highly-polished style. Meanwhile that same style, for Wordsworth, is the root of a complacent vanity that deflects Pope away from properly poetic subjects (such as nature) and towards self-serving fame. The larger inference is that certain types of form or content – social satire, rhyming couplets, 'polish', 'logic' – will lead to showy, sterile, or excessively commercial writing. In other words, verse not poetry.

These insinuations retain their influence. The heroine of Sylvia Plath's *The Bell Jar* (1963) hates 'the very idea of the eighteenth century, with all those smug men writing tight little couplets and being so dead keen on reason'.[33] And note Plath's dismissal of a poetic rival: 'Light verse: she's sold herself'.[34] For Plath, the choice seems to be between male smugness and female superficiality. Insofar as this is a choice between rhyming couplets and 'light verse', the eighteenth century is implicated in both options. Oddly, though, Plath could herself be presented as an occasional writer. Poems such as 'Burning the Letters', 'The Arrival of the Bee Box' and 'Words heard, by accident, over the phone' (all from 1962) are, in a strict sense, occasional: they commemorate specific happenings. Indeed the first of these poems, with its 'carbon birds',[35] bears interesting comparison to the 'vain atoms' and 'fatal relics' of Sarah Dixon's rather less well-known 'Lines Occasioned by the Burning of Some Letters' (1740; *EWP* 178).

In presenting Plath's work as an extreme instance of occasional poetry, I don't mean to ignore the differences between her and the poets who form the subject of this book; her work springs from, and addresses, a different context. However I do think it's instructive that we have difficulty imagining Plath and Dixon in the same sentence. Specifically, why is the eighteenth-century poet 'occasional' (with all that that implies) while the twentieth-century one is not? The answer lies in the intensity of Plath's poetic voice. Her persona courts mythic effects by identifying itself with the Holocaust and the bombing of Hiroshima. Whatever one thinks of this move, the scope of the identification amounts to a bid for sublimity (as opposed to what Plath represents as the commercialism of 'light verse'). Moreover, Plath brings comparable fierceness to relatively mundane scenarios such as bonfires and telephone conversations. Indeed that's why she's such a preeminent exponent of romantic discourse.

Of course Plath's heightened register would not have been easily available to eighteenth-century women poets. Towards the end of the century, Charlotte Smith wrote an influential series of sonnets featuring sublime locations, and Ann Radcliffe's poetry is marked by the sublime touches that also characterize Radcliffe's Gothic fiction. However many women would have echoed Priscilla Pointon's claim to be 'not sublimed', especially if they were writing earlier in the eighteenth century. For example, there's a comparable refusal of sublimity, plus a response to sexual difference, in Mary Leapor's 'Upon her Play being returned to her, stained with Claret'. Leapor was a domestic servant whose *Poems Upon Several Occasions* were published by posthumous subscription in 1748. (She died of measles in 1746, aged 24.) The poem's title refers to an unsuccessful attempt, on the part of Leapor's patron, to have one of Leapor's plays produced in London. Welcoming her 'dear wanderer' back to its 'native cell', Leapor's narrator speculates on her manuscript's travels in the masculine world of theatrical producers:

But say, O whither hast thou ranged?
Why dost thou blush a crimson hue?
Thy fair complexion's greatly changed:
Why, I can scarce believe 'tis you.

Then tell me, my son, O tell me, where
Didst thou contract this sottish dye?
You kept ill company, I fear,
When distant from your parent's eye.

Was it for this, O graceless child!
Was it for this you learned to spell?
Thy face and credit both are spoiled:
Go drown thyself in yonder well.

The carelessly stained text embodies literary culture's powerful indifference to working-class women writers. Like the prodigal son, the manuscript must stop seeking its fortune abroad; it belongs with its creator, not with the theatrical gate-keepers who have used it ill. And by extension, Leapor herself has been told not to aspire too highly; for, as the poem puts it, 'The Court was never made, I'm sure / For idiots like thee and I' (*EWP* 211–2).

Although the poem registers the difficulty, for a working-class woman, of becoming literate, let alone of being published, Leapor's tone remains wryly satirical. Her wit does not defuse the poem's underlying anger. Instead it channels the anger into a self-mocking register that dares the reader to accept the narrator at her own estimation. Are the play and its author as idiotic as Leapor claims? Or should we attend, instead, to the skill with which the poem is controlled, and to the air of sardonic self-sufficiency that seems to contradict the narrator's self-deprecation? The difficulty of answering these questions definitively is indicated by the couplet I've just cited. When Leapor writes that the court wasn't intended 'For idiots like thee and I' (rather than 'thee and *me*'), is she making an unwitting grammatical error, is she ignoring grammar in order to make her rhyme scheme work, or is she using the error to draw attention to the paucity of her formal education?

While this issue can't be resolved, the poem eschews the unsettled feelings that Burke, Kant and Lyotard associate with sublimity: the poem's indeterminacy doesn't produce a crisis of selfhood. And while Leapor uses the staining of the manuscript to make points about class and gender, she refuses to over-freight the occasion; if anything, she underplays it for humorous effect. Despite such modesty, 'Upon her Play being returned to her' is a sophisticated poem. Or rather – to make a crucial distinction – the poem's modest air is part of its sophistication. This isn't the sophistication of the sublime, but it's nonetheless an artful mode in which modesty (or the appearance of modesty) helps invoke a more homely – but equally valid – world of blushes, stains and child-rearing. Like the poem's humorous register, these household touches evoke a poetic ethos that's been lost, or that only survives in forms that are ignored by the critical mainstream. Moreover, such changes in fashions have been driven, at least in part, by anxieties about gender. If the poem's tone and content could be typed, in a general sense, as 'feminine' it's because Leapor emphasizes interior space. And the domestic, of course, is not sublime.

The comparison that I've drawn between Plath on one hand, and Leapor and Pointon on the other, suggests an interconnection between scale, sublimity and gender. Plath magnifies her poetic persona by identifying with moments of global destruction. In doing so, she projects domestic and personal occurrences (such as childcare and marital breakdown) into a sublime register that would have been unimaginable to her eighteenth-century predecessors. As part of this process, Plath collapses different time periods into each other. To take a specific instance, the first-person speaker of 'Fever 103°' lays claim both to the moment of composition (October 20, 1962) and to various earlier moments, notably the death of Isadora Duncan on September 14, 1927, and the bombing of Hiroshima on August 6, 1945. By contrast, eighteenth-century occasional poetry usually speaks to, or tries to capture, singular occurrences. Nor should this be surprising, because 'occasions' by their nature are historically defined.

More than that, 'occasions' are bound into time in ways that challenge idealist definitions of poetry. In other words, as I've argued throughout this chapter, occasional works tend to thwart romantic and New Critical constructions of poetry as a heightened form of communication. They do this both by featuring concrete objects and by containing moments rather than trying to transcend them. There is, therefore, a fourth concept to place alongside my discussions of scale, gender and sublimity: time. In the next (and final) section of this chapter I want to link these threads together by asking how romantic and postmodern accounts of sublimity and time affect attitudes to occasional poetry. In particular, I'm interested in how Lyotard uses the sublime to investigate 'what Martin Heidegger called *ein Ereignis*' that is, 'an event, an occurrence' in which 'thought must be disarmed'.[36] I will then link this to the gendering of the sublime and the occasional.

## TIME AND GENDER

As we've seen, Lyotard's account of the sublime stresses experiences that overwhelm expression. By bearing 'expressive witness to the inexpressible', sublime phenomena make possible the question that Lyotard places at the heart of avant-garde expression, namely 'Is it happening?'[37] In one sense 'Is it happening?' is simply another version of the indeterminacy that Lyotard values in the avant-garde and the sublime. Ultimately, however, Lyotard's question concerns a particularly extreme form of indeterminacy in which consciousness – or even existence – falls into doubt. This is what Lyotard means by the sublime 'event' in which time, and the event itself, are called into question.

Here Lyotard is again following an eighteenth-century cue, namely Burke's contention that 'fear' more than any other passion 'robs the mind of ... its powers of acting and reasoning', and that the fear that sublimity produces resembles 'actual pain' and, is linked, ultimately, to death.[38] For Lyotard, the 'major stake' in Burke's aesthetic is 'the threat of nothing further happening' – the fear, that is, of death itself. According to this reading, the sublime emotion occurs when a powerful object deprives the 'soul' of its usual sense that something else is about to happen. Within the resultant oscillation of pain and delight, the sublime emerges not as 'a matter of elevation [as it would have been for classical writers such as Longinus] ... but a matter of *intensification*'.[39]

These observations seem far removed from the issues raised by 'Upon her Play being returned to her, stained with Claret'.

It's not only that Leapor's poem investigates a relatively banal occurrence – the staining of a manuscript, not the climbing of a treacherous mountain, or the destruction of the World Trade Center on September 11, 2001. (An occurrence that Jean Baudrillard described as 'the absolute event... the pure event uniting within itself all the events that have ever taken place'.)[40] It's also that Leapor's wit – which has implications of control, as well as of humour – limits the incident's dramatic possibilities: in Lyotard's terms, the poem refuses the intensification associated with sublime immeasurability.

That said, Leapor's poem does engage with time. Like most occasional poems, its title advertizes its origin in a specific moment. This is further underlined by the title of the book in which it appears: *Poems on Several Occasions*. However there is obviously a difference between Leapor's conception of time and the much grander claims that Lyotard makes for 'the event'. Unlike 'the occasional', 'the event' disrupts linear time in ways that produce ahistorical or transcendent effects – hence Baudrillard's notion that the destruction of the Twin Towers united 'within itself all the events that have ever taken place'. By definition, the bounded 'occasion' is less thrilling than Lyotard's expansive 'event' but that doesn't mean that we should accept the inherent superiority of a sublime aesthetic. (Although neither should we simply replace the sublime with the occasional.) Instead I want to suggest that an unquestioning acceptance of the sublime blocks our understanding and appreciation of pre-romantic poetry because it obscures the different sorts of 'value' found in the occasional. For example, Leapor's poem is of worth not because it asks 'Is it happening?' but because it tells us that something has happened. Moreover the 'occasion' that it records has had, and will continue to have, a measurable impact on Leapor's status: since the play has been rejected, its author must continue in service.

The philosophical tradition from which Lyotard is writing warns that terms like 'time', 'history' and 'identity' should not be taken for granted. I acknowledge that deconstruction is right to question received versions of what it means, or how it feels, to be alive but I am anxious about the quasi-religious plenitude/ desolation that marks certain strands of postmodern thought, especially when it comes to sublimity. For example, what does

Lyotard mean when he says that art returns 'the soul' (*l'âme*) to an 'agitated zone between life and death'?[41] Leaving aside the argument that art is an ideological category that should be treated with scepticism, one might ask what souls have got to do with Lyotard's analysis. Has Lyotard unhesitatingly accepted Burke's eighteenth-century vocabulary, or is he slipping into a strange kinship with W. K. Wimsatt? Although their reference points are different, Wimsatt and Lyotard share a taste for quasi-divine transcendence, even if Lyotard finds it in the unbounded whereas Wimsatt looks to the self-contained. As a consequence, both commentators generate overwhelmingly formalist readings, although they look for different things in their favoured texts.

I'm additionally troubled by Lyotard's 'soul' because it encourages less guarded writers to embrace baroque religiosity. Lyotard isn't oblivious to materialist politics: his essay on the sublime and the avant-garde notes how easy it is for the avant-garde to be neutralized as a result of its own commodification. However in Baudrillard's hands, postmodern sublimity becomes synonymous with the collapse of enlightenment logic at the hands of a mystical nihilism. 'Logic' is a legitimate target for deconstructive scepticism but if we have to abandon our trust in 'reason', must we therefore accept a vacuous apocalypse in which insight becomes impossible? By writing that 'the World Trade Center Event' defies 'any form of interpretation', Baudrillard rejects both critical analysis and the possibility of change. Instead he falls into an unexamined identification with nineteenth-century romanticism – hence the echoes of F. W. Nietzsche in Baudrillard's contention that we need to 'look beyond Good and Evil' because 'Western philosophy' naïvely believes in 'the progress of Good' and therefore fails to understand that 'Good and Evil advance together, as part of the same movement'.[42] As a by-product of this march, the world is locked in a system of 'terror against terror' in which 'there is no longer any ideology'. Instead 'we are far beyond politics and ideology'.[43]

Baudrillard is right to confront his readers with the possibility that September 11 was a desired 'event', an occurrence that produced a global transference in which television viewers compulsively consumed a spectacle that was both 'real' and 'symbolic', and that was also bizarrely similar to the epic disasters of the US film industry. But by refusing to build on the space opened up by this provocative assertion, Baudrillard passes up an opportunity to explore, say, the sublime impulse behind Harlan Ullman's *Shock and Awe: Achieving Rapid Dominance*, a military handbook published in 1996 by Washington's National Defence University Press. Ullman's views, which were enacted in the Second Gulf War, advised the Pentagon to destabilize future enemies via high profile strikes on key targets: in theory, victory could be achieved more quickly and with fewer personnel than through an old-fashioned invasion of the enemy's borders. The 'shock and awe' of Ullman's title is a version of Burke's and Kant's sublime because military power is being used as a demoralizing spectacle that will destabilize individuals and the communities of which they are a part. However Baudrillard pursues neither the sublime roots of this tactic nor its implications for a history of sublime.

If nothing else, Ullman's book reminds us that the sublime is not only an aesthetic category; political forms of sublimity go back at least as far as the French Revolution. Burke's *Reflections on the Revolution in France* (1790) uses sublime effects to support the status quo; by contrast, Jacobin revolutionaries stage-managed the execution of aristocrats in order to produce sublime horror. One hardly needs add that the technologies of modern warfare are sublime in a peculiarly potent, if cold-blooded, way. The link to poetry and gender comes when we remember that the sublime – like warfare – is gendered as masculine. And so, too, are certain genres and registers of poetry. For example at the beginning of *The Task*, Cowper questions both epic poetry and the martial versions of masculinity that it often inscribes. Echoing the opening of the *Aeneid*, Cowper changes Virgil's 'I sing of arms and the man' to 'I sing the Sofa'. Sofas indicate leisure, relaxation and middle-class gentility. They do not imply warfare or sublimity.

Cowper's mock-heroic stance also projects his poem into female space – note the many scenes from eighteenth-century novels where heroines rest, faint or flirt on sofas. The poem's 'Advertisement' acknowledges this context when it explains that 'a lady, fond of blank verse, demanded a poem of that kind from the author, and gave him the SOFA for a subject'. Working on the challenge, Cowper found that 'his situation and turn of mind' led him to produce 'a serious affair' rather than 'the trifle which he at first intended' (*PWC* ii, 113). The result might be termed the apotheosis of occasional poetry: a six-book work sparked by a piece of furniture. Epic in scale but modest in tone, the poem's shift from martial masculinity to female domesticity is reinforced both by the circumstances of its composition and by its 'occasional' form. For the three years preceding the publication of *The Task*, Lady Austen had been Cowper's muse, walking companion, and prospective marriage partner. Although their association ended acrimoniously before the poem appeared, the friendship can be seen as a trial run for the poet's smoother relations with Harriot Hesketh, who re-entered Cowper's life shortly afterwards. By extension, *The Task* resembles the poems to Hesketh that I discussed in Chapter 2. Like them, it emerges from the poet's flattering attentions to a better-off, titled woman; and it, too, juxtaposes material objects with discussions of poetic identity. In both cases, the poet occupies an interior sphere that's more usually associated with women; and women, of course, provide the financial and emotional environment from which the poetry emerges.

Cowper's identification with female space has a negative effect on his posthumous reception because literary history comes to prefer what Keats calls the '[W]ordsworthian or egotistical sublime'. As 'a thing per se' that 'stands alone', Wordsworth's 'egotistical sublime' does not give way before other people. Instead, it is the medium through which Wordsworth mediates the external world. By contrast, Keats's account of his own 'poetical Character' describes a poet who 'has no Identity' because 'he is continually... filling some other Body'. Rather than asserting a presence, Keats effaces himself through multiple identifications: 'When I am in a room with People ... the identity of every one in the room begins [so] to press upon me that, I am in a very little time an[ni]hilated – not only among Men; it would be the same in a Nursery of children'.[44] Unable to stand a glance from that most 'romantic' of objects – a child – Keats evokes a mixture of pleasure and pain similar to the psychic disorganization that Burke and Lyotard find in those who view the sublime. (There are obvious parallels here to Cowper's terror of public speech and his fear, in Olney, of being overseen by neighbours.) By comparison Wordsworth's singular ego is itself a sublime edifice, hence Wordsworth's ability to construct a poetic voice of literally epic proportions.

Keats's self-diagnosis has been coarsened by commentators eager to use him as a feminized and infantilized foil to Wordsworth. Remarking on Keats's 'complete enervation', Matthew Arnold complains that one of his letters 'has in its relaxed self-abandonment something underbred and ignoble, as of a youth ill brought up, without the training which teaches us that we must put some constraint upon our feelings and upon the expression of them'.[45] Like Arnold's comments on Pope, this view of Keats has become an enduring prejudice: as recently as 1995, Paul Fry stated blankly that 'We know perfectly well from both the poetry and the life that the combination of prolonged adolescence, fear of rejection, small stature, and the sexual hectic that goes with fevers confused Keats even beyond the Regency norm about women'.[46] Unsurprisingly, Arnold's model poet is Wordsworth, who turns out to be the epitome of mature masculinity – and sublime to boot. Placing Wordsworth above every English poet except Shakespeare and Milton, Arnold holds that Wordsworth 'deals with *life*, as a whole, more powerfully' than his rivals. Moreover, his 'poetry is precious because his philosophy is sound'. And – in an interesting touch – his productivity is itself valuable: even laying aside his weaker poems, he produced an 'ample body of powerful work'.[47]

These judgements are, of course, ideological: they reveal literary history's bias towards middle-class masculinity.[48] (Arnold also accuses Keats of writing like a surgeon's son.) But such processes are important to my argument about occasional poetry because, as John Dolan shows, Wordsworth avoids the taint of occasional writing by re-conceptualizing the form. And although Dolan doesn't pursue a gendered analysis, Wordsworth's reformulation of literary tradition is almost certainly informed by a wish to re-masculinize the poetic sphere. As Roger Lonsdale argues, Wordsworth's definition, in the 'Preface' to the *Lyrical Ballads*, of the poet as 'a man speaking to men' is calculated to claw territory back from the female poets and readers who had sprung up in the latter half of the eighteenth century.[49] Wordsworth's rhetorical erasure of women's writing is accompanied by a simultaneous appropriation of the space that female and working-class poets had begun to occupy – for theirs are the voices that he ventriloquizes in many of his contributions to the *Lyrical Ballads*. Consequently, a male, educated, middle-class voice is allowed prominence over a multiplicity of emerging female voices, many of them working- or lower-middle class – and none of them, of course, Cambridge graduates (as Wordsworth was).

This process also entails the expulsion, from literary respectability, of the domestic world that most working-class and women poets wrote about. Concrete or utilitarian examples of occasional poetry become downgraded in favour of poems on art objects or on the sublimity of nature. (And here we should remember that respectable women could not experience 'nature' – whether sublime or otherwise – unless they were chaperoned: an unaccompanied woman on a country road was as good as a prostitute.) Interventions such as Wordsworth's and Arnold's mean that the occasional becomes typed as limited, concrete, banal and untranscendent. By no coincidence it is also defined as female and domestic, which contrasts sharply with the ways in which contemporary theories of 'genius' stressed sublime originality – a quality that was overwhelmingly associated with men.[50] This move has an obvious effect on the reputations of writers such as Leapor, Yearsley and Pointon. In tandem, it affects male poets, such as Gray and Cowper, who experiment with the gendered possibilities of occasional writing.

Since I have already mentioned Cowper's flirtation with triviality (and his implied mockery of martial masculinity) in the opening of *The Task*, I now want to shift the discussion towards Gray. Although both poets have been typed as effeminate, the accusation is sparked by different kinds of misdemeanour. In Cowper's case, commentators have seemed anxious about his fondness for non-sexual female friendships: he is deemed too close to the world of the sofa. But as a Fellow of a Cambridge college, Gray's world was overwhelmingly male. Moreover, as I will argue in the next chapter, Gray's sexual identity was demonstrably homoerotic in a way that Cowper's wasn't.[51] In preparation for that discussion, I want to note that the 'Preface' to the *Lyrical Ballads* doesn't only erase female poets. It also – in a related move – attacks Gray's 'Sonnet on the Death of Mr Richard West'.

In one of the most famous parts of the 'Preface', Wordsworth claims that only five lines of Gray's poem have 'any value' – the rest being marked, like most of Gray's work, by 'curiously elaborate...poetic diction'. Instead Wordsworth recommends 'the language really spoken by men'. Wordsworth does not remark on the content of Gray's poem, or its form. Had he done so, he might have noted that sonnets had long been out of fashion, and that Gray was one of the first to resurrect the form. (Wordsworth, Coleridge and Keats would follow.) The genre's lack of vogue may or may not have been connected to the homoeroticism of Shakespeare's sonnets. In any case, before the form was taken up by Wordsworth and the later Romantics, it had mostly been used by eighteenth-century women writers such as Charlotte Smith and Mary Robinson.

Wordsworth also seems oblivious to the fact that Gray's sonnet – as its title indicates – is a mourning piece in which one man laments the loss of another. But although Wordsworth ostensibly ignores the poem's subject matter, his choice of text seems far from accidental given his insistence on 'the language really spoken by men'. The implication is that Gray's sonnet fails to speak man's proper language. The further implication – and this may explain Wordsworth's defensive tone – is that poetry itself is feminine whereas prose is masculine: hence Wordsworth's claim, throughout the 'Preface', that 'the language of every good poem can in no respect differ from that of good Prose'.[52] We are left to infer that unpretentious, manly prose is needed to protect poetry from the wiles of an overly 'poetic' diction. Ironically, though, Wordsworth's 'Preface' is itself highly rhetorical – 'artificial', indeed; as such, it undermines Wordsworth's claim that the language of prose is more transparent than that of poetry.

As Arnold's commentaries show, Wordsworth's rhetoric lays the ground for a canon that aspires toward masculine plain speaking but that threatens constantly to collapse into immaturity or effeminacy. Although Arnold places Wordsworth at the apex of modern poetry, this vision requires Arnold to acknowledge Gray and Keats as lesser figures, poets who fail to be as manly or as productive as the author of *The Prelude*. Paradoxically, however, this highlights the very failings that Arnold is warning against. The result is a shadow-canon in which Gray

71

and Keats can be identified as major influences on Alfred Tennyson – who, by no coincidence, was also much troubled by anxieties about masculinity. Tennyson lies well outside the scope of this book, but attentive readers will doubtless find links between his work and that of Thomas Gray – the main subject of my next chapter. Accordingly, I now want to explore some eighteenth-century versions of a discourse that is central to Gray's work, and that would later be important to Keats, Shelley, Tennyson and (in a different way) Walt Whitman. I refer, of course, to the pastoral.

# 4

## Homoeroticism
## and the Pastoral

There is no intrinsic reason why shepherding should be a popular subject for literary writing: why herdsmen and not schoolteachers? Yet pastoral motifs show an astonishing ability to survive and mutate. Classical and renaissance writers viewed the pastoral as the oldest form of poetry and the genre's continuing power is demonstrated by the commercial and critical success of Ang Lee's 2005 film of E. Annie Proulx's 1997 short story 'Brokeback Mountain'.[1] Unfortunately, commentary on pastoral poetry has tended to emphasize formal and literary-historical patterns over the political contexts in which the genre has flourished.[2] And although Raymond Williams, James Turner, Roger Sales and John Barrell have analysed the class connotations of pastoral writing,[3] relatively little has been said about the eighteenth-century pastoral's engagement with homoeroticism. This is odd given that same-sex desire is as prominent in classical and renaissance pastorals as it is in Lee's *Brokeback Mountain*. Moreover gender and sexuality are closely linked to the pastoral's role in the construction and projection of poetic identity.

The present chapter will extend this book's investigation of form and ideology by exploring how male eighteenth-century pastoral poets elide or exploit the form's ancient preoccupation with homoerotic desire; it will also ask what these poetic responses tell us about changing constructions of masculinity. The discussion will culminate in a reading of the eighteenth century's most famous pastoral poem, Thomas Gray's 'Elegy Written in a Country Churchyard'. But before looking at Gray, we need to understand why the pastoral occupied such a powerful place in the eighteenth century's literary imagination. It's not only that pastoral writing offered an apparently nostalgic and idealized version of the past, it's also that the pastoral's otherworldly space frequently refers – directly or indirectly – to contemporary society. The pastoral was therefore a genre in which allegories of the present could be enfolded within fantasies of the past.

To give a specific instance, pastoral poetry often comments on the relationship between clients and their patrons; thus, critics have often argued over the degree to which Virgil's *Eclogues* (42–37 BC) do or do not praise the poet's patron, Augustus Caesar. In addition, the genre gains prestige from its ability to trace such controversies beyond Virgil, to the Greek poet Theocritus, who wrote in the third century BC. This long history flattered the poets and patrons of later days so that if an eighteenth-century writer imitated Virgil he was implying that his protector was a modern-day Augustus (although without the tyrannical tendencies). These analogies also operated on a national scale. By styling itself 'Augustan', early eighteenth-century metropolitan culture laid claim to the imperial, as well as the literary, aspirations of Augustus's Rome. This necessitated some sleight of hand. For instance, James Thomson's *Liberty* (1735–6) traces the eponymous goddess's flight from Greece, to Rome, and finally to Britain. In doing so, the poem represents the classical world as corrupt (hence Liberty's need to take refuge in Britain) and as noble (hence Britain's wish to inherit Rome's mantle). Thomson reconciles these imperatives by distinguishing between the Roman Republic (which he upholds as chastely moral) and the Roman Empire (which he uses to warn Britain against over-consumption). Other writers put Rome to different uses.[4] But whatever the agenda, eighteenth-century neo-classicism was rarely arbitrary. On the contrary, writers placed themselves in a political arena every time they echoed Virgil and Horace or imitated genres such as the pastoral or the verse epistle.

Crucially for this chapter, the versifying shepherds who populate pastoral poetry allegorize literary production in ways that inform subsequent accounts of creativity. By mythologizing the origins of poetic speech, these all-singing, all-piping workers promote reflections on poetry's functions, as well as on the world of power in which writing is formed and through which it circulates. It's no accident that a singing competition is a standard component of the classical pastoral. Famous versions of this trope can be found in Theocritus's fifth *Idyll* and Virgil's third *Eclogue*. In both cases, two herdsmen trade poetic insults while a third party decides whose voice is the more effective. Such contests comment on the rivalries produced by patronage, as well as on the individual poet's longing for recognition. As such, they enact the connection between poetry, politics and economics that I traced in Chapter 2.

By extension, these singing competitions also encapsulate the pastoral's role in constructing and transmitting literary hierarchies. In other words, because poets sought to establish their value through the pastoral, the entire genre can be seen as a trans-historical singing competition in which symbols of poetic achievement (such as lyres and pipes) are passed across the generations. Thus, eighteenth-century writers used the pastoral to assert their kinship with a tradition that stretched through William Shakespeare, Sir Philip Sidney and Edmund Spenser to the Greek and Roman poets who shaped the genre. Given this, it's no coincidence that Alexander Pope's first published work was an adaptation of Virgil: his *Pastorals* of 1709 consist of short poems on each of the seasons plus an essay in which he identifies the *Eclogues* as his major model. Pointedly, Pope's 'Summer' has Edmund Spenser passing his rustic flute to a poet called 'Alexis'. The flute stands for lyric poetry while 'Alexis' echoes Pope's first name (*PAP* 130). It further strengthens Pope's claim on poetic authority that 'Alexis' is also the name of a character in Virgil – albeit a rather problematic one. (More of which anon.)

With typical modesty, Pope claimed to have written his *Pastorals* at sixteen.[5] This is itself a formulaic gesture: aspiring poets frequently used the pastoral as a staging-post on the way to longer, even more prestigious forms, such as the epic. Pope was not alone in apprenticing himself to the pastoral: the early work of Milton, Blake, Byron, and Keats includes adaptations of pastoral conventions such as the piping shepherd, the evening star that guides the worker home, and the absent friend mourned by fellow herdsmen. Feminist critics have shown that these devices are not exactly suited to female use; and nor does pastoral poetry bear much resemblance to the 'reality' of country life. For though some pastoral texts register emigration and poverty,[6] many others persist in idealizing the rural economy. Indeed Pope's *Discourse on Pastoral Poetry* (1709) claims that since the form 'is an image of what they call the Golden Age' it is better 'not to depict shepherds as shepherds at this day really are, but as they may be conceiv'd then to have been'. Furthermore it is necessary to use 'some illusion to render a Pastoral delightful' and this consists of 'exposing the best side only of a shepherd's life, and in concealing its miseries' (*PAP* 120).

Such insouciance was harder to maintain as the eighteenth century proceeded: industrialization, the enclosure of common land, changes in agricultural practice, and the enlargement of cities all had negative effects on already constrained rural lifestyles. These pressures are registered in poems such as Oliver Goldsmith's 'The Deserted Village' (1770) in which a recently lost golden age is evoked to reveal the inequities of the present. Later, Wordsworth's 'Michael' (1800) would challenge urban readers to rethink their attitude to the countryside. Subtitled 'A Pastoral Poem', 'Michael' is a story of rural depopulation and family loss in which a faithful worker's sheepfold is left unfinished at his death because his only son has been corrupted by city life. At the time of publication, much of the poem's power would have come from the gap between the pastoral's idyllic associations (as indicated in the subtitle) and Wordsworth's depiction of a doomed rural economy.

At the same time that social change remodelled the country and the city, commentators such as Jean-Jacques Rousseau were expounding what has come to be known as primitivism. By emphasizing 'nature' over 'culture', primitivism downplayed the over-educated middle and upper classes in favour of people and objects that were deemed unspoilt and unsophisticated. Key primitivist figures included rural workers, children, the illiterate, non-western subjects (including the enslaved), and women. So while there's a sharp contrast between primitivism and the self-conscious literariness of the pastoral, it would be dangerous to see one as 'natural' and the other as 'artificial'. In truth, both discourses are highly constructed. Although primitivism stresses the unsophisticated, it can only do so from a position of educated authority. Thus, the pastoral presents implausibly leisured swains singing of unrequited love while primitivism romanticizes working-class illiteracy. Neither is very helpful to 'actual' rural workers.

Moving from class to gender, we find that primitivism privileges women for biological rather than intellectual reasons: being close to nature meant giving birth and breastfeeding, it didn't mean reading or writing. It was therefore easier for women to be the objects of primitivist discourse than for them to be agents in public life. By prizing emotional responses rather rational debate, the related discourse of sensibility corralled women into physical rather than verbal articulacy. Thus, sensibility emphasized blushing, crying and fainting rather than literary production. Chapter two of this book used Ann Yearsley's reception as an example of how women could both use, and fall victim to, primitivist versions of the pastoral. The rest of this chapter will take an allied route through this territory by analysing the homoerotic possibilities of the pastoral.

## SAME-SEX DESIRE AND THE PASTORAL

In 1772 William Kenrick published an ironic defence of the 'Platonic love' that 'burns with undistinguish'd rage, / And spares in fondness neither sex nor age'. (A 'love', that is, that turns to younger men as well as to women.) Tracing this unregulated desire to the ancient world, Kenrick asks why minor 'errours' should be turned into 'crimes' when the greatest writers of Greece and Rome had themselves had sex with younger men.

> Must not the taste of Attic wits be nice?
> Can antient virtue be a modern vice?
> The Mantuan bard, or else his scholiast lies[,]
> Virgil the chaste, nay Socrates the wise,
> The gay Petronius, sophists, wits and bards,
> Of old, bestow'd on youth their soft regards; [...]
> Could lightenings ever issue from above
> To blast poor men for such a crime as love[?][7]

Kenrick's mockery reveals a faultline in Augustan Britain. Politicians and writers who identified with the military and cultural reach of Augustus's Rome had to find ways of explaining

or evading classical poetry's intermittently homosexual config-
urations. The pastoral was particularly suspect because its two
most famous exponents, Virgil (Kenrick's 'Mantuan bard') and
Theocritus, produced unambiguously homoerotic poems. More-
over if the pastoral was the ancient font from which all other
poetry sprang, then perhaps poetic utterance actually derived, in
part, from male-on-male desire. After all, the original singing
match was between two male ex-lovers.[8]

Given that sodomy was a capital offence in eighteenth-
century Britain, it's easy to see why many poets responded to
these difficulties by changing the love object's gender when
they adapted homoerotic texts. Take Virgil's second *Eclogue*
where the shepherd Corydon addresses his unloving colleague,
Alexis. We've already seen that Pope turns this poem to his
advantage by claiming 'Alexis' as an echo of his own name,
Alexander. Crucially, though, Pope's imitation excises Corydon
and makes Alexis the speaker (rather than the object) of the
poem. As well as removing a homoerotically-identified character
from the original, this ensures that Pope's textual persona
expresses desire for a woman, not a man. In a comparable move,
Pope's *Discourse on Pastoral Poetry* complains that Theocritus's
fourth and fifth *Idylls* contain 'abusive and immodest' characters
(*PAP* 121). This view was long-lasting: Cambridge University
Press's 1950 translation of Theocritus switches from English to
Latin at key moments of the fifth *Idyll*, thus protecting non-
classically educated readers from the full nature of Comatas the
goatherd's relationship with the shepherd Lacon. (Comatas
buggers Lacon against an oak tree.)[9]

By their nature, cultural faultlines have mixed effects. While
some writers were repelled or inhibited by classical homoeroti-
cism, others may have embraced the pastoral precisely because
it lent classical legitimacy to dissident desires. Richard Barn-
field's *The Affectionate Shepherd* (1594) is a case in point: the 'I' of
his poem confesses love for 'a sweet-fac'd Boy' whose 'amber
locks' frame 'his lovely cheeks with joy'.[10] Although Barnfield's
directness is all but unmatched in the English pastoral tradition,
other writers used the form to explore the ambiguities of male
friendship. A key instance is Edmund Spenser's *The Shepheardes
Calendar* (1579), where Colin loves Rosalind but is himself
pursued by another man, Hobbinol.

Glossing Spenser's 'Januarye', the mysterious editor E. K. notes:

> In thys place seemeth to be some savour of disorderly love, which the learned call pæderastice: but it is gathered beside his meaning. For who that hath red Plato may easily percieve, that such love is muche to be alowed and liked of, specially so meant, as Socrates used it: who sayeth, that in deede he loved Alcybiades extremely, yet not Alcybiades person, but hys soule, which is Alcybiades owne selfe. And so is pæderastice much to be præferred before gynerastice, that is the love whiche enflameth men with lust toward woman kind. Yet let no man thinke, that herein I stand with Lucian or hys develish disciple Unico Aretino, in defence of execrable and horrible sinnes of forbidden and unlawful fleshinesse. Whose abominable errour is fully confuted of Perionius, and others.[11]

Here E. K. (who may or may not be Spenser himself) contrasts two types of male-male relationship. One is preferable to the love of women while the other is an 'unlawful fleshliness' – but the text does not tell the reader how to navigate the space between the two.

Writers searching for a specifically English canon were drawn, throughout the eighteenth century, to *The Shepheardes Calendar* and *The Faerie Queene* (1590–6) because Spenser's studied archaisms presented a bridge between contemporary culture and the medieval past. Amongst many others, Pope, Thomson, Wordsworth, Shelley, Keats and Coleridge used Spenserian references to place themselves within a self-consciously national tradition. Given Spenser's importance in the construction of 'English poetry', and given the pastoral's role in generating representations of a 'native' landscape, it's striking that *The Shepheardes Calendar* writes same-sex desire into the English pastoral in such a conspicuous (if ambiguous) way. And even though commentators are divided on how to read E. K.'s glosses, the poem undoubtedly preserves the homoeroticism that Pope would later omit from his pastoral works.

Two decades after Pope's *Pastorals*, Thomas Gray showed himself more open to Virgil's same-sex possibilities. Tellingly, though, Gray's private letters are more forthright than his published poetry. Writing to his school friend Horace Walpole in 1736, Gray creates an all-male rural retreat through classical allusion.

I live with my Uncle, a great hunter in imagination...he holds me mighty cheap I perceive for walking, when I should ride, & reading when I should hunt...My comfort amidst all this is, that I have at the distance of half a mile thro' a green Lane, a Forest (the vulgar call it a Common) all my own...[I]t is a little Chaos of Mountains & Precipices; Mountains it is true, that don't ascend much above the Clouds, nor are the Declivities quite so amazing as Dover-Cliff, but just such hills as people, who love their necks as well as I do, may venture to climb...[B]oth Vale & Hill is cover'd over with most venerable Beeches, & other very reverend Vegetables, that like most ancient People, are always dreaming out their old Stories to the Winds

> And, as they bow their hoary Tops, relate
> In murm'ring Sounds the dark Decrees of Fate;
> While Visions, as Poetic eyes avow,
> Cling to each Leaf, & swarm on ev'ry Bough:

At the foot of one of these squats me I; il Penseroso, and there grow to the Trunk for a whole morning,

> – the tim'rous Hare, & sportive Squirrel
> Gambol around me –

like Adam in Paradise, but commonly without an Eve, & besides I think he did not use to read Virgil, as I usually do there: in this situation I often converse with my Horace aloud too, that is, talk to you; for I don't remember, that I ever heard you answer me; I beg pardon for taking all the conversation to myself; but it is your own fault indeed. (*CTG* i, 47–8; the quatrain is Gray's.)

Walpole would have recognized Gray's 'squatting' under the 'most venerable Beeches' as a mock-heroic version of the opening of Virgil's first *Eclogue* where the farmer Tityrus contemplates nature from under a beech tree. (As we'll see, this scene recurs in Gray's writing.) Walpole may have heard Gray's 'sportive Squirrel' as an echo of Book Four, lines 340–5 of *Paradise Lost* and he would certainly have known that the 'Il Penseroso' with which Gray identifies himself is an early Milton poem that celebrates rural melancholy. More pointedly, the ending of Gray's letter recalls Virgil's second *Eclogue*. There the solitary Corydon addresses his unloving male friend Alexis just as Gray, faced with Walpole's absence, takes 'all the conversation to myself'. Meanwhile the 'Horace' to whom Gray speaks is both Horace Walpole and the Roman poet whose works Gray is reading. Furthermore, Gray's allusions to Milton and 'Adam in

Paradise' recall the Garden of Eden, the ultimate Christian pastoral. However Gray's paradise lacks an Eve. Instead he replaces the mother of the human race with Horace Walpole: a witty transposition that restores the pastoral's same-sex dynamic.

Gray's circle of friends provides ample evidence of how classically literate writers (almost always men) could evolve – or possibly confirm – alternative selves through pastoral allusion.[12] Thus, four months after his letter to Walpole, Gray was urged by another school friend, Richard West, not to

> throw poetry 'like a nauseous weed away'. Cherish its sweets in your bosom, they will serve you now and then to correct the disgusting sober follies of the common law, misce stultitiam consiliis brevem, dulce est desipere in loco; so said Horace to Virgil, those sons of Anac in poetry, and so say I to you, in this degenerate land of pigmies,
>
> > Mix with your grave designs a little pleasure
> > Each day of business has its hour of leisure.
>
> > (*CTG* i, 57–8)

Here, too, a fizz of literary prototypes is cited in support of romantic friendship. The closing couplet loosely translates the Latin from the preceding paragraph. The source is an ode in which Horace invites Virgil, his friend and fellow poet, to abandon seriousness for a visit of playful relaxation;[13] the poem also alludes to Arcadia, a familiar pastoral location. By comparing Gray to Virgil, and himself to Horace, West links male friendship, poetic aspiration and the classics. In effect, he is telling Gray that despite the depths to which society has fallen, the friends might re-kindle something of the Golden Age by banding together. (The sons of Anac – or Anak – are giants from the Bible; they are also mentioned in Milton's *Samson Agonistes*.)[14]

Communications such as these may seem remote from twenty-first century readers, turning as they do on an effortless exchange of fairly arcane knowledge. Latin, however, was an essential component of an eighteenth-century gentleman's education: Gray and his circle are enacting their gentility by trading classical allusions. But as my discussion of Cowper in Chapter 2 showed, gentlemanly postures need financial support. Horace Walpole had no fears on that score: his father

81

was the enormously rich (and famously corrupt) Prime Minister, Sir Robert Walpole. Gray and Richard West had more modest backgrounds. West's father and uncle were lawyers; Gray's father was a scrivener and his mother and aunt ran a millinery shop. Both men would have been expected to earn their own living.

Although it would be ridiculous to present Gray and West as underprivileged, they certainly couldn't live out their cultural preoccupations in the way that Walpole would when he converted a Twickenham villa into England's most famous mock-Gothic building, Strawberry Hill. Instead Gray achieved a more off-the-peg correspondence between his inner and outer landscapes by becoming an intermittently depressed Cambridge don. The pastoral's mixture of the bucolic, the fanciful, and the power-driven was thus available on a daily basis by the banks of the Cam. That, however, was still in the future. As students, he and West were restricted to what they could achieve on paper.

The letter in which Gray addresses Walpole from underneath a beech tree is a good example of such textual reinvention. I've already noted the letter's richly allusive tone, but what about the physical landscape it evokes? The 'little Chaos of Mountains & Precipices' in which Gray places himself is an imagined scene. That is, Gray's Virgilian pose gives him the literary perspective ('Poetic eyes') that can turn a 'Common' into a 'forest'. However, as the letter acknowledges, Gray has no power to impose this transfigured world on other people. On the contrary, he can only grant himself centrality in letters and poems. Elsewhere the contemplative artist has been disenfranchised in favour of 'the vulgar' (who see a 'Common' not a 'forest') and of men like Gray's uncle who would rather hunt than read.

For all its cleverness and verve, the letter hints that isolation may be the price you pay for poetic imaginings: there's a thin line between loneliness and inspiration, especially if you are talking to someone who isn't there and are surrounded, instead, by people who don't understand you. Perhaps the letter also admits that 'the Vulgar' have the comfort of a shared perspective: by definition, they outnumber Gray's classically-literate friends. Consequently, the world operates more through their eyes than his. Gray returns to this theme in the 'Ode on the

Spring', which I'll discuss in a moment. But first I want to note that Gray's other main correspondent, Richard West, also shows what one might call a defensive contempt for 'the vulgar'.

Studying at Oxford, West refers to university as a 'dismal land of bondage' adding that 'an inn of court [where lawyers trained] is as horrid a place as a college' (*CTG* i, 57). This is loaded given his family's links to the law, and given that West himself was bound unhappily for the profession. Comparable dissatisfaction appears in an earlier letter to Gray, where West pictures himself at school

> hand in hand with you, like the two children in the wood,
>
> > Through many a flowery path and shelly grot,
> > Where learning lull'd us in her private maze.
>
> The very thought, you see, tips my pen with poetry, and brings Eton to my view. Consider me very seriously here in a strange country, inhabited by things that call themselves Doctors and Masters of Arts; a country flowing with syllogisms, where Horace and Virgil are equally unknown. (*CTG* i, 33–4)

The Eton of the early-eighteenth century was notoriously boorish: Gray and West weren't straightforwardly happy there. West hints as much by picturing himself and Gray holding hands for comfort in the forest, like the children in Charles Perrault's 'Little Thumb' (1697).[15] But this allusion also shows that Eton could be re-imagined, and made bearable, through literary analogues.

Sadly, life after school was less malleable. That's why West prefers Eton to the 'strange country' of adulthood where male friends cannot walk hand in hand, even in imagination. His university studies are a collection of meaningless formulas, unlike the classical learning of his schooldays, which are a wellspring of both romantic friendship and literary production: just thinking about the 'private maze' of 'learning' brings Eton, and poetry, into West's head. However the resultant pastoral is also erotic: note the phallic implications of West's pen being tipped with poetry. Compare Gray's reference elsewhere to 'the vast abundance & volubility of M^r Walpole & his Pen' (*CTG* i, 114). And consider, too, why 'learning' should propel one into a 'private maze'. Why private and not public? Indeed why a maze at all?

Here, as often, the Gray/West letters reveal a complex inter-penetration between male friendship, poetic aspiration, desire, and the pastoral. Seeking to be both poets and friends, Gray and West exchange translations, new compositions, and allusions until their lives become bound together by texts that explore and express their attachment – texts, indeed, that help create that attachment. But as with E. K.'s glosses on *The Shepheardes Calendar*, it is difficult for participants and observers to know where male friendship ends and sexual desire begins – hence the tetchiness with which William Mason, Gray's literary executor, insisted that Walpole excise the pet names from his and Gray's correspondence. Referring to these pastoral tags, Mason complained of 'the infantine beginnings and conclusions [of some of the letters] which are hardly fit for schoolboys and yet will not be considered as written by a schoolboy'.[16]

Gray would investigate this territory in the 'Elegy Written in a Country Churchyard' and the 'Sonnet on the Death of Mr Richard West'. But before discussing these poems, I want to examine the social implications of Gray's preference for pastoral writing. In particular, how would the non-literary world have gendered his and West's preference for childhood ties over adult responsibility?

## PASTORAL RETIREMENT AND MASCULINE IDENTITY

Gray's and West's rejection of business, politics and the law follows the example of Horace, whose so-called 'retirement' to a farm in the Sabine hills was a model for poets wishing to withdraw from civic life. More recently Pope had set up a famous villa (complete with grotto) in the then village of Twickenham. Such choices played into long-standing construc-tions of the country as morally pure and the city as corrupt. However that does not mean that Pope, or indeed Horace, were abdicating their right to address public affairs. On the contrary, their retirement authorized them to comment critically on metropolitan power structures. What's more, they justified their retirement by writing prolifically.

Gray, however, wrote relatively little poetry, and his work rarely concerns the factional politics that Pope routinely dissects in his satires. Instead Gray uses retirement to muse on internal dilemmas. This self-absorption triggers anxieties, in himself and his audience, about masculinity because as the eighteenth century went on, poetry became increasingly associated with escapist evasions of male public duty. As John Sitter notes

> By the mid-century, retirement has hardened into retreat. The poet characteristically longs to be not only far from the madding crowd...but far from everybody. Accordingly, many of the poems that most reflect the 1740s and 1750s are not epistle – that is, not poems with an explicit audience and implicit social engagement – but soliloquies or lyrics, usually blank verse musings or odes addressed to personifications.[17]

This could be a direct account of Gray's poetic *oeuvre*. Not only does his work abound with odes and personifications, it is highly self-referential, and the implied audience – where there is one – tends to be highly specialized. Indeed on at least two occasions, his addressee is dead. (I discuss these below.)

Note, too, Gray's resistance to public displays of learning. Having spent six years lobbying to be made the Regius Professor of Modern History at Cambridge, the adult Gray found himself unable to deliver any lectures. The ensuing anxiety produced a nervous collapse that's comparable in type, though not degree, to Cowper's breakdown after failing to give evidence before the committee that was going to examine his right to a government sinecure. Gray's refusal of public speech is echoed by his poetry, much of which contrasts touchstones of masculinity (public life, forthright utterance, heterosexual love) with problematic varia-tions on them (retirement, silence, male friendship). Take the 'Ode on the Spring', which Gray enclosed in a letter to West in 1742. At first the poem's speaker views the outer world with contempt: 'How low, how little are the proud / How indigent the great!' (GCG 51). The narrator's morally superior tone seems justified because he (unlike 'the great') has chosen pastoral retirement.

Like many of Gray's letters, the poem signals this rustic preoccupation by echoing the overhanging beech trees of Virgil's first *Eclogue*: 'Where'er the rude and moss-grown beech / O'er-canopies the glade /.../ With me the Muse shall sit, and think' (GCG 50). Importantly, these lines emphasize thought not speech ('With me the Muse shall sit and think'). The speaker goes on to argue that reflection is better than action because in the eyes of 'Contemplation' the 'race of man' looks like a hoard of insects who 'shall end where they began' (GCG 52). Consequently, worldly aspiration is fruitless. However the poem also resembles the letter (cited above) in which Gray places himself at the centre of a transfigured landscape, only to find that no one shares his perspective. Thus, the 'Ode on the Spring' gives the last word, not to the insights gained by pastoral retirement, but to the outside world's scorn at those who have chosen silent inactivity. As his condescension falters, the narrator finds he no longer believes his own rhetoric.

> Methinks I hear in accents low
> The sportive kind reply:
> Poor moralist! and what art thou?
> A solitary fly!
> Thy joys no glittering female meets,
> No hive hast thou of hoarded sweets,
> No painted plumage to display:
> On hasty wings thy youth is flown;
> Thy sun is set, thy spring is gone –
> We frolic, while 'tis May.
>
> (GCG 53)

The 'sportive kind' silence the 'Poor moralist' by revealing his inadequate life, including his rejection of conventional romance ('Thy joys no glittering female meets'). Significantly, though, this sceptical voice does not come from outside the poem. Rather, it is a product of the moralist's self-doubt ('Methinks I hear in accents low / The sportive kind reply'). Thus the poet provides a dismissal of his own position, and allows that dismissal to close the poem. By undercutting its own narrative voice, the 'Ode on the Spring' questions both the pastoral and the kinds of masculinity that the form generates. But since it also exposes the futility of 'the great', the poem leaves its speaker without a clear model.

Unsatisfied with both retirement and activity, the 'Ode on the Spring' is the almost inevitable product of Gray's and West's difficulty in reconciling classical learning with the need to earn a living. Gray's 'Ode on a Distant Prospect of Eton College' (written 1742, published 1747) is equally uncertain about the transition from youthful innocence to adult responsibility. The 'prospect' of the title is both spatial (the view from Gray's uncle's home to his old school) and temporal (the view from later life back to childhood). Like Gray's and West's letters, the poem idealizes Eton: its playing fields are a pastoral paradise where 'once my careless childhood strayed / A stranger yet to pain' (*GCG* 57). However adult knowledge ushers in a Fall. Thus, through a battery of personifications, the poem argues that the 'ministers of human fate' and 'Misfortune's baleful train' will educate their 'little victims' by informing them of their future unhappiness.

Significantly, their fate is gendered. Or rather, gender is their fate:

> Ah, show them where in ambush stand
> To seize their prey the murtherous band!
> Ah, tell them, they are men!

(*GCG* 60)

These lines suggest there's nothing arbitrary about the Eton/Eden pun that runs through the Gray/West correspondence. It's not just that Gray's and West's ejection into adulthood echoes Adam and Eve's expulsion from paradise. It's also that both departures produce a newly crippling sense of sexual difference. Leaving behind an all-male, adolescent space for a world in which two men cannot hold hands while discussing the classics, Gray and West reconstruct Eton as a lost paradise. There, at least, it was unnecessary either to marry or to have a professional identity. So even if the 'real' Eton was less idyllic, it remained preferable to adulthood for, as Jean Hagstrum puts it, being a man, in Gray's world, 'is, with fatal inevitability, to be melancholy'.[18]

Poetic retirement could be justified if the resultant poetry dealt patriotically with trade or public morality. That was how William Cowper excused his retreat from active masculinity; it also worked for James Thomson. However Gray seeks a more emotional connection to the outside world. Driven by its origins in romantic friendship, Gray's pastoral poetry upholds sympathetic identification. Thus, the 'Eton' ode says that although all men are 'condemned alike to groan', the 'tender' will groan 'for another's pain' while the 'unfeeling' groans 'for his own' (*GCG* 63). The 'Ode To Adversity' (written 1742, published 1753) has a similar resolution. As its title suggests, the poem features another set of ghoulish personifications, including 'screaming

87

Horror's funeral cry, / Despair and fell Disease and ghastly Poverty'. But although these are undeniably horrid, Adversity can also be called upon 'To soften, not to wound my heart' (*GCG* 73). As in the 'Eton' ode, such softening is educative. The speaker therefore asks Adversity to

> Teach me to love and to forgive,
> Exact my own defects to scan,
> What others are to feel, and know myself a man.
>
> (*GCG* 74)

The syntax of the middle line is characteristically knotty: paraphrased it means, 'Examine my defects closely'. Gray chooses to invert the line (putting the adverb before the verb) so that he can match 'scan' with 'man', thus finishing the poem with a clear-cut rhyme. Significantly, the single-stress words that close these lines are known, technically, as 'masculine' endings.

Together these effects place enormous force on the word 'man' while also drawing attention to the final line's distinction between knowledge and feeling. 'Know thyself!' is one of Enlightenment culture's great cries: Pope's *Essay on Man* (1733–4) closes 'And all our Knowledge is, OURSELVES TO KNOW' (*PAP* 547). Although Gray echoes this sentiment, his poem is more specifically about gender knowledge. That is: the speaker feels for other people but he must know himself a man. So while sympathy helps him identify with other people's emotions ('What others are to feel'), he himself needs intellect not sentiment ('and know myself a man'). This suggests that the narrator has to monitor his behaviour for proof of an adult – and masculine – identity. The further implication is that you cannot simply be a man, you also have to check you're acting out the appropriate roles. By extension, your manliness may be called into question if you feel *too much*.

Gray's challenge is to construct a poetic identity that registers the anguish of male adulthood without resorting to a withdrawal into solitude. The 'Eton' and 'Adversity' odes do this by replacing the egocentricity of the 'Ode on the Spring' with a general concern for humanity. However Gray's most famous poems – the 'Elegy Written in a Country Churchyard' and the 'Sonnet on the Death of Mr Richard West' – showcase the affective ties that form between particular friends. As well as showing the limitations of an undifferentiated sympathy, these works place male friendship at the heart of the pastoral tradition. As such, they're the poetic embodiment of themes that Gray had earlier explored in his correspondences with Richard West and Horace Walpole.

## UNRAVELLING GRAY'S 'ELEGY'

For a poem that could plausibly claim to be the most anthologized in the English language, Gray's 'Elegy' is curiously hard to read. Featuring three voices arranged like Chinese boxes, the poem's conclusion complicates what seems initially to be a serene evocation of rural England. Although my reading focuses on this complex final section, I want begin with the poem's overall structure: an extended treatment seems appropriate given the text's cultural significance.

The 'Elegy' begins with evening casting the narrator into solitude:

> The curfew tolls the knell of parting day,
> The lowing herd wind slowly o'er the lea,
> The ploughman homeward plods his weary way,
> And leaves the world to darkness and to me.

> (GCG 117)

After two stanzas of general observation, the narrator turns to the churchyard of the title, noting that 'Beneath those rugged elms [...] / The rude forefathers of the hamlet sleep' (GCG 120). The next three verses reflect the dead's separation from the rural scene they once inhabited: 'The cock's shrill clarion or the echoing horn, / No more shall rouse them from their lowly bed' (GCG 121). Then the narrator muses more generally on human aspiration and the inevitability of death: no matter whom you are, 'The paths of glory lead but to the grave' (GCG 124). This perspective is reinforced by a series of personifications (Memory, Honour, Flattery, Death) that recall the threatening figures in Gray's 'Eton' and 'Adversity' odes.

At this point – a third of the way through the 120 line poem – the narrator changes tack, asking if the occupants of the rural graveyard might have had different lives had they dwelt elsewhere.

Perhaps in this neglected spot is laid
Some heart once pregnant with celestial fire;
Hands that the rod of empire might have swayed,
Or waked to ecstasy the living lyre.

But Knowledge to their eyes her ample page
Rich with the spoils of time did ne'er unroll;
Chill Penury repressed their noble rage,
And froze the genial current of the soul.

(*GCG* 125–7)

That is: if it hadn't been for poverty and illiteracy some of the villagers might have been poets or politicians. Here, and in the stanzas that follow, Gray lays aside Pope's advice that poets should ignore the realities of rural life. Instead Gray reminds the reader that people like the ploughman who 'homeward plods his weary way' are constrained by the very structures (economic, educational and regional) that render them picturesque to metropolitan observers.

Gray's sympathetic awareness of class contrasts with Cowper's tendency to see the illiterate as insensate animals. However that doesn't mean that Gray has a radical agenda. On the contrary, although rural obscurity may have robbed the country of a great poet ('Some mute inglorious Milton here may rest') it also protects the villagers from violent hubris ('Some Cromwell guiltless of his country's blood'), (*GCG* 128). Gray pursues this idea in some of the poem's most famous lines:

Far from the madding crowd's ignoble strife
Their sober wishes never learned to stray;
Along the cool sequestered vale of life
They kept the noiseless tenor of their way.

(*GCG* 131)

Lack of opportunity may be morally advantageous.

Turning to the churchyard gravestones, the narrator notes that even the most obscure villager has 'some frail memorial'. However these markers also bear witness to poverty and illiteracy: the inscriptions, which are written by the 'unlettered muse', feature 'uncouth rhymes' and 'shapeless sculpture'. Like all such monuments, these seek a sympathetic response from later viewers; or, as the poem puts it, they '[implore] the passing tribute of a sigh' (*GCG* 132). These sighs recall the appeals to fellow-feeling in the 'Eton' and 'Adversity' odes. The 'Elegy' goes further, though, in arguing that the dying need a specifically loving attendant rather than generalized sympathy:

> On some fond breast the parting soul relies,
> Some pious drops the closing eye requires;
> Ev'n from the tomb the voice of nature cries,
> Ev'n in our ashes live their wonted fires.

> (GCG 133–4)

This thought is now developed at length through the story of a rural poet whose alienation from society ends when he dies young.

Although the 'Elegy' has been building towards this point, the poet's story is introduced in a challengingly complex way. In particular, something baffling is about to happen to the narrator's voice. Immediately after the stanza quoted above, the narrator starts addressing himself rather than the reader. In other words, having earlier referred to himself in the first person singular ('And leaves the world to darkness and to *me*'), he now uses the second person singular ('thee') to describe his role in narrating the poem: 'For thee who, mindful of the unhonoured dead, / Dost in these lines their artless tale relate' (GCG 135). The effect is both puzzling and electrifying, especially as the narrator goes on to tell himself what might happen if 'some kindred spirit' enquired about his fate in the way that he has enquired about the people buried in the churchyard. In answer, he imagines an old labourer ('some hoary-headed swain') recounting the story of a doomed poet-figure who wandered the countryside distractedly.

Taken from the start, the narrator's transition from the first person to the second reads as follows:

> For thee who, mindful of the unhonoured dead,
> Dost in these lines their artless tale relate;
> If chance, by lonely Contemplation led,
> Some kindred spirit shall inquire thy fate,

> Haply some hoary-headed swain may say,
> 'Oft have we seen him at the peep of dawn
> Brushing with hasty steps the dews away
> To meet the sun upon the upland lawn'.

> (GCG 135–6)

The next four stanzas recall – or rather foretell – the poet-figure's sickness and abrupt disappearance. The first of these verses provides yet another echo of the beech trees under which Tityrus muses at the start of Virgil's first *Eclogue*:

> 'There at the foot of yonder nodding beech
> That wreathes its old fantastic roots so high,
> His listless length at noontide would he stretch,
> And pore upon the brook that babbles by'.

(GCG 136–7)

However, unlike the would-be complacent speaker in the 'Ode on the Spring', this man is disturbed. The 'hoary-headed swain' describes how

> 'Hard by yon wood, now smiling as in scorn,
> Muttering his wayward fancies he would rove,
> Now drooping, woeful wan, like one forlorn,
> Or crazed with care, or crossed in hopeless love'.

Although we can guess what lies ahead, the wanderer's death is not described within the poem. Instead, the swain's story jumps from the poet's sudden absence to a funeral procession that appears some days later:

> 'One morn I missed him on the customed hill,
> Along the heath and near his favourite tree;
> Another came; nor yet beside the rill,
> Nor up the lawn, nor at the wood was he;
>
> The next with dirges due in sad array
> Slow through the church-way path we saw him borne'.

(GCG 137)

So ends the story of the 'crazed' poet-figure. However the poem itself has another twist.

Having finished his tale, the swain tells the narrator to read the inscription on the dead man's tombstone ('Approach and read (for thou canst read) the lay, / 'Graved on the stone beneath yon aged thorn'). Although the swain registers the educational gap between himself and the narrator '(for thou canst read)', the poem ends neither with his voice nor that of the literate narrator. Instead it closes with a three stanza 'Epitaph' written in the anonymous, unpolished register that the narrator had earlier associated with rustic churchyard monuments. This is the first stanza of the 'Epitaph' (all of which is italicized in the original):

> *Here rests his head upon a lap of earth*
> *A youth to fortune and to fame unknown.*
> *Fair Science frowned not on his humble birth,*
> *And Melancholy marked him for her own.*

(GCG 138-9)

Taken as a whole, then, the poem's final nine stanzas offer a structure in which the narrator's calmly observant voice is overtaken by the swain's, and where the swain in turn gives way to the 'Epitaph'. (Which, by its nature, is silent: it's made of stone.)

Although these devices seem to remove the narrator from his own poem, he himself has instigated his disappearance. The story of the man who dies before his time was prompted, remember, by the narrator asking himself how he will be recalled after death. The brooding figure under the beech tree is therefore an imagined version of his own future, just as the epitaph is a self-description. The first book devoted to Gray's work, *Designs by Mr R. Bentley for Six Poems by Mr T. Gray* (1753), conveys this with graphic brilliance. Bentley's frontispiece for the 'Elegy' shows the narrator leaning toward the headstone of the rural poet until his shadow fills the grave. Meanwhile the swain points him (and us) toward the epitaph.[19]

## MALE FRIENDSHIP AND THE 'ELEGY'

The Augustan narrator's transformation into an obscure rural poet illustrates, once more, the futility of worldly ambition. The poem's structure enacts its leading theme: the man who comments on other people's graves will, in his turn, be silenced by death. But while Gray's 'Elegy' obviously has much to say about human aspiration, it should be evident also that it is a poem about male friendship. This becomes more apparent in the second stanza of the 'Epitaph':

> *Large was his bounty and his soul sincere,*
> *Heaven did a recompence[sic] as largely send:*
> *He gave to Misery all he had, a tear,*
> *He gained from Heaven ('twas all he wished) a friend.*

(GCG 139-40)

Here, the generalized sympathy of the 'Eton' and 'Adversity' odes is directed toward a specific object – thus fulfilling the narrator's comment in lines 89–90 that 'On some fond breast the parting soul relies, / Some pious drops the closing eye requires'.

I will say more about the rural poet's friend in a moment, but first I want to note that much critical anxiety has focussed on the supposed 'badness' of the poem's closing verses. Some readers have preferred an earlier draft of the 'Elegy' in which there is no mention either of the swain or the 'Epitaph'. (Gray added these elements during the revision process.). In response, one could argue that the awkwardness of the 'Epitaph' embodies the poem's emphasis on private relations over worldly success: a more polished style might miss the point. But even if one accepts that argument, there's still a tension between the published ending and what Roger Lonsdale calls the 'classical or "Augustan" restraint and balance' of the original draft. Although Lonsdale prefers the revised poem, he concedes that the earlier one may be more 'balanced and lucid' (*GCG* 114–5). Trying to account for these changes, Lonsdale notes that the expanded version gives a more complex account of the relationship between poetry and society. Thus, for Lonsdale, the alienated figure in the swain's story is a metaphor for the poet-as-outsider; meanwhile the 'Epitaph' shows that the sensibility which estranges the poet from society may also be emotionally nurturing.

However this reading raises a possibility that Lonsdale himself does not canvas, namely that the poem exceeds its own form. By this I mean that the qualities most associated with Augustan writing – balance, elegance, and classical restraint – cannot accommodate the message introduced by the less balanced and elegant 'Epitaph'. By giving way to an 'unlettered muse', the narrator seems to concede the pastoral's limitations – or the limitations, at least, of the version he has inherited. According to this interpretation, the conclusion's clumsiness is the undesired but inevitable outcome of an attempt to push the eighteenth-century pastoral further than it wants to go. (This is what I mean when I say that the poem exceeds its own form.) In particular – and this is where formal issues link with homoerotic themes – the conclusion's linguistic strain may be linked to the relationship between the rural poet and the 'friend' who

94

supplies his emotional wants – '*He gained from Heaven ('twas all he wished) a friend*'.

I'm struck, for example, by the brackets that proliferate in the poem's final section. Besides the line I've just quoted, they appear in the swain's introduction of the tombstone: 'Approach and read (for thou canst read) the lay'. In these instances, the brackets clarify the poem's thought: they make snappy observations about rural illiteracy and male friendship. Such clarity is notably lacking, however, in the poem's final stanza, which lays the rural poet to rest with the words

> *No farther seek his merits to disclose,*
> *Or draw his frailties from their dread abode,*
> *(There they alike in trembling hope repose)*
> *The bosom of his father and his God.*

(GCG 140)

The bracketed third line drives such a wedge between lines two and four that the meaning only emerges after repeated readings. (We shouldn't pry any further into the dead man's good and bad points since all his qualities now reside, in hope and trepidation, with God in heaven.) And even then uncertainty remains. Far from introducing an illuminating aside, this parenthesis raises questions about the content of the line and the rebarbative way in which it's been expressed. Why, for example, does this most quoted of poems end with a stanza that is, literally, unspeakable? (Although I have known the 'Elegy' for most of my adult life I remain incapable of reciting its last stanza successfully.) It's as if there's something here that cannot be said, or even thought, but that nonetheless disrupts the poem's tone – something that short-circuits the poem's expected resolution. But if we accept this insight, we have to find a way of exploring that something – or somethings – without forcing through a single, reductive interpretation.

Faced with this difficulty, it's helpful to remember Pierre Macherey's notion that gaps and absences reveal the ideological tensions that inhabit every text.[20] Reading for silences can be a way of activating unacknowledged meanings – meanings that derive, moreover, from history's pressure on the text. This last point is important because Macherey is less interested in the psyche of the author than in the proposition that texts emerge in tension with historical forces, not all of which are known to, or controllable by, the writer, and some of which may produce opposite effects to the ones intended by the author. Following Macherey, the final stanza of the 'Elegy' could be heard as a stutter, a hesitation that retrospectively casts doubt on the poem's previous assurance. This stutter can be heard in different ways but I want to suggest that one response would be to hear it as a clash between pastoralism and Christian morality.

These components need not be in direct opposition: post-classical poets often imported Christian themes into pastoral poetry. For example, early Christian commentators read Virgil's fourth *Eclogue* as a prediction of Christ's coming. (The poem promises the birth of a child who will usher in another Golden Age.) Dante's *Divine Comedy* (*c*.1307–21) is, amongst other things, an extended gloss on this idea: Virgil appears as a character who guides the pilgrim poet through Hell and Purgatory until Beatrice, the embodiment of Christian wisdom, whisks the pilgrim up to Heaven. An important English instance is Milton's 'Lycidas' (1637), a pastoral elegy in which a dead herdsman is raised by Jesus, the ultimate Good Shepherd. However these antecedents integrate pastoralism and Christianity more seamlessly than Gray's 'Elegy'. 'Lycidas' is conceived from start to finish as a Christian allegory. But as we've seen, Gray changes the emphasis of the 'Elegy' by adding the swain, the alienated poet and the 'Epitaph' to what was previously a much more conventional meditation on the vanity of human aspiration.

Although these additions re-state the poem's morality, they also introduce less controllable associations. In particular, the added stanzas emphasize a peculiarly exclusive version of male friendship. Given that Gray was a professing Christian, there's no reason to doubt the sincerity of the poem's conclusion. But it's nonetheless striking that the 'Elegy' falters when it hopes that the dead poet will rest peacefully in the *'bosom of his father and his God'*. (Even interior readings struggle to make this verse coherent; it falls completely apart when spoken aloud.) This drop into silence hints at a conflict between the pastoral genre's partially buried homoeroticism and Gray's avowed morality. When the two collide, the 'Elegy' becomes, in a literal sense, unreadable. This is unsurprising given the homoeroticism of Gray's letters. It's not just that the classical pastoral is more prominent than Christianity in Gray's correspondence. It's also that Gray's version of the classical tradition edges him toward what E. K. (in his glosses on *The Shepheardes Calendar*) calls 'execrable and horrible sinnes of forbidden and unlawful fleshinesse'. The terrain is especially risky because both the letters and the 'Elegy' stress particular friendships. In 'Lycidas', Milton's subject and narrator are part of a larger community of shepherds, but the poet in the 'Elegy' has only one defence against alienation: the single friend who is 'all he wished' from 'Heaven'.

There are other ways of reading the fissure at the end of Gray's 'Elegy' – for instance George Haggerty finds a sexual shudder in the poem's reference to 'trembling hope'.[21] But in looking for the thing, or things, that disrupt the poem it is important not to rush, prematurely, to define Gray or his work through late-nineteenth-century sexology. As well as assuming that later homosexual/heterosexual identities can be transferred into the eighteenth century, this approach drives out the very ambiguities that Gray exploits, to literary and emotional effect, in his writing. So while I'd argue that Gray's personal life was dominated by his relations with West, Walpole, and a couple of subsequent male friends, I'd look for other ways of contextualizing those relationships. One of sexology's more obvious short-comings is that it creates categories that are more rigid than our actual subjectivities. Gray's investment in male friendship therefore offers an extra-literary reason for prizing his writing, namely that his work embodies an otherwise lost way of loving. More than that, his writing challenges us to reconsider the protective boundaries we have learnt to draw between the friendly and the erotic. (Haggerty's *Men in Love* makes a valuable contribution to exactly this project.)

Similarly, while I'd contend that Gray's friendships both form, and were formed by, his literary activities, I wouldn't argue that the pastoral is a cover for more explicit communications. Rather, Gray and West gravitate to the pastoral precisely because key examples of the form cross back and forth between friendship and desire. Thus the genre's instability echoes and confirms male friendship's instability. In this reading, the 'something' that unhinges the 'Elegy' isn't incidental. Instead, it's central both to the poem and the larger tradition from which the poem emerges. This is related to my earlier point that the faultlines in pastoral writing make the form both attractive and repellent to writers who are interested in same-sex desire. In all these cases the pastoral becomes available as a palimpsest on which larger cultural forces are inscribed. Or, to put the thought more strongly, the pastoral becomes one of the key discourses in which those forces are renegotiated by writers and readers.

## THE AFTERLIFE OF RICHARD WEST

Earlier in this chapter, I noted that Gray sent the 'Ode on the Spring' to West in 1742. However I did not mention that the letter containing the poem was returned to Gray unopened. It was only through a newspaper item that Gray learnt what his friend's family did not think to tell him, namely that West had died of consumption. He was twenty-five. Although the unread letter brings Gray's correspondence with West to an abrupt end, Gray's bereavement becomes the engine for some of his most important work. In this final section of the chapter, I want to use West's continuing presence to reveal the patterns of saying and unsaying that characterize Gray's writing. In doing so, I want to repel Matthew Arnold's assessment of Gray as the poet who 'never spoke out'.

Worrying about Gray's output, Arnold notes that 'He was in his fifty-fifth year when he died, and he lived in ease and leisure, yet a few pages hold all his poetry how shall we explain his scantiness of production?'[22] These terms reveal poetry's implication in capitalism: Arnold is genuinely baffled at Gray's failure to use his 'ease and leisure' to create poetic commodities. (By contrast, Arnold is impressed by the bulk, as well as the quality, of Wordsworth's *oeuvre*.) But instead of pathologizing Gray as the poet who 'never spoke out' I want to argue that Gray's work choreographs speech and non-speech to produce what one might call resonant silence. This phenomenon is exemplified by the loaded ways in which the narrators of the 'Elegy' and the 'Ode on the Spring' disappear from their own poems. 'The Bard' (1757) performs a more dramatic version of the same gesture: having said what he wants to say, the eponymous bard throws himself off a cliff top.

98

These manoeuvres dramatize poetry's ambiguous place in mid-eighteenth-century culture. Can the classically-inflected lyric make itself heard in a world increasingly dominated by prose fiction? But Gray's primary audiences are personal: his poems circulate in letters long before they reach a wider public. (Having fruitlessly sent the 'Ode on the Spring' to West, Gray waits another six years before publishing the poem in one of Robert Dodsley's anthologies, and even then he acts at Walpole's instigation.) Comparisons to William Cowper suggest that Gray's reticence is connected to general uncertainty about how gentleman poets should behave in the literary marketplace. But cultural anxieties about speech are only part of the picture. There is also the literal silence that greets the poem when Gray sends it to West, the co-creator of his pastoral milieu.

The force of West's death is evident from another fractured text, Gray's Latin poem *De Principiis Cogitandi*, which deals with the importance of touch in John Locke's philosophy. The poem's first book had been produced in consultation with West, who is identified as its intended audience ('For the work is produced for you');[23] it is also dedicated to him. However West's death changes the poem from a philosophical treatise to an elegy: 'But now you, the inspiration and cause of so great a task, have deserted me in the midst of it and have hidden yourself in the eternal shadow of Death'.[24] Consequently, 'my only wish is to mourn at your tomb and address these empty words to your silent ashes'.[25] By breaking off, unfinished, the poem makes the reader hear the difference between Gray's speech and West's silence. In doing so, the poem asks what it means (and how it feels) for words to go unspoken or unheard.

The bereaved poet's address to his friend's unspeaking remains anticipates the final portion of Gray's 'Elegy', in which the swain confronts the narrator (and the reader) with the tombstone of the 'crazed' rural poet. Given that the alienated bard is a representation of the narrator, it makes more sense to identify the rural poet with Gray rather than with West. However that in itself produces a tribute to West. By noting that the dead writer gained 'a friend' and that this is 'all he wished', the 'Epitaph' acknowledges West's place in Gray's heart. Moreover, this identification illuminates something that would otherwise remain unclear, namely why the rural poet dies alone. The swain's story implies that the rural poet has somehow lost his friend and sees no point in living without him – and this inference is strengthened if we know about Gray's and West's friendship.

Commentators differ on whether the 'Elegy' was a direct response to West's death; and I would not want to reduce the poem to its biographical circumstances. However I do think it significant that the silences to which I've drawn attention are in dialogue with a particular form of 'saying', namely Gray's borrowings from West's unpublished poems. By using West's words in his own poetry, Gray gives the dead man's ashes a voice. (This is an example of what I call 'resonant silence'.) Gray's use of West's poem 'Ad Amicos' is especially interesting. When West sent the poem to Gray in 1737, he explained that it had been inspired by a combination of a 'melancholy elegy' by Tibullus and one of Pope's letters to Richard Steele. West uses these sources to summon up an entirely male scenario in which he, languishing in Oxford, addresses Gray and Walpole in Cambridge. They are the 'happy youths' who 'feel each joy that friendship can divide' whereas he is a 'sad exile in a desert land'. Unlike his old schoolmates, he has no friends who can 'mix their heart with mine' while sharing 'mutual warmth'.

Although West's language is highly constructed, his poem insists on emotional openness. He disowns literary ambitions, claiming that his lines are 'all devoid of art' and only have value because they 'give back the image of my heart'. He strikes a similar note while introducing the poem, saying that while it cannot 'divert' his friends, it will at least 'show them how sincere' he is (CTG i, 61–2). The ending restates emotional values. Whatever the quality of the verse, there are some people

> Within whose breasts my tomb I wish to raise[...]
> To them may these fond lines endear,
> Not from the poet but the friend sincere.

> (CTG i, 64)

In other words, West wants to bury himself in his friends' hearts so that they can be his living memorials ('Within [their] breasts my tomb I wish to raise'). This overturns the more conventional expectation that poets will be memorialized through their writing.[26]

West's emphasis on sincerity is echoed in Gray's letters, and in the 'Elegy', which places a comparable emphasis on sincere friendship over literary fame:

> Large was his bounty and his soul sincere,
> Heaven did a recompence[sic] as largely send:
> He gave to Misery all he had, a tear,
> He gained from Heaven ('twas all he wished) a friend.

> (GCG 139–40)

In this stanza, tears demonstrate the rural poet's emotional transparency. West's request for sincere affection is therefore heard and reproduced in the language of the 'Elegy'. What's more, Gray's account of sincere emotions is framed – like West's – within a complex linguistic edifice. That is: the 'Epitaph' that contains the poem's declaration of love and loss is folded within the less emotionally available voices of the narrator and the swain. Taking this thought further, the 'Epitaph' can be seen as a verbal equivalent of the 'tomb' that West wants to raise for himself within his friend's heart. Unable to create a literal monument, Gray erects an imaginary gravestone at the climax of his most famous poem, and in doing so he demonstrates that he, too, has a 'soul sincere'. As a result, as an earlier section the 'Elegy' puts it, 'Ev'n from the tomb the voice of nature cries, / Ev'n in our ashes live their wonted fires' (GCG 134).

Gray also echoes West's 'Ad Amicos' at the climax of 'The Bard',[27] but his most prominent use of the poem is in the 'Sonnet on the Death of Mr Richard West'. In 'Ad Amicos', just before the passage where he hopes that his friends will enshrine him in their hearts, West worries that

> Few will lament my loss whene'er I die [...]
> The world will pass as chearful as before,
> Bright as before the day-star will appear,
> The fields as verdant, and the skies as clear;
> Nor storms nor comets will my doom declare
> Nor signs on earth, nor portents in the air;
> Unknown and silent will depart my breath,
> Nor Nature e'er take notice of my death

> (CTG i, 63)

As this extract shows, West's poem is both an individualized plea for sympathy and a comment on pastoral discourse. The fields may be green and the weather fine but that's not much good when you're dead (and nor, by extension, is the pastoral poetry that places such store on outdoor life).

Gray's 'Sonnet on the Death of Mr Richard West' expresses an even stronger scepticism about pastoral poetry: the poem describes a mourning so profound that its speaker is untouched by the rebirth of the natural world. Significantly, however, the 'Sonnet' reproduces the language of West's 'Ad Amicos' in order to insist that West *is* mourned, despite nature's indifference. Indeed, the dead man and his bereaved friend are united, in their different states, by nature's indifference to both of them.

> In vain to me the smiling mornings shine,
> And red'ning Phoebus lifts his golden fire:
> The birds in vain their amorous descant join,
> Or cheerful fields resume their green attire:
> These ears, alas! for other notes repine,
> A different object do these eyes require.
> My lonely anguish melts no heart but mine;
> And in my breast the imperfect joys expire.
> Yet morning smiles the busy race to cheer,
> And new-born pleasure brings to happier men:
> The fields to all their wonted tribute bear;
> To warm their little loves the birds complain.
> I fruitless mourn to him that cannot hear,
> And weep the more because I weep in vain.
>
> (GCG 67–8)

Gray did not publish these lines during his life – they were presumably too private – but they were much discussed after they appeared in William Mason's 1775 edition of Gray's poetry. As we saw at the end of the last chapter, Wordsworth attacked the sonnet's diction in the 1800 'Preface' to the *Lyrical Ballads*. More recently, the poem has appeared in *The Penguin Book of Homosexual Verse* (1986).

I want to end with the 'Sonnet', partly because it demonstrates West's fundamental place in Gray's literary life, but also because it comments so astutely on the limitations, as well as the possibilities, of pastoral writing. The poem rehearses familiar motifs – birdsong, the movement of the sun across the sky, the busy beauty of the pastures – only to show what inadequate responses these are to human loss. In doing so, the poem exposes both the necessity and the futility of literary writing. By attempting to perform the very consolation that it tells us is impossible, the poem makes that consolation available, at least in principle, to subsequent readers. But insofar as the poem is specifically about the pastoral (rather than about literary writing more generally), it returns the genre to its homoerotic origins while demonstrating – via Wordsworth's negative response – that those origins are unwelcome within the developing canon of 'English Literature'. (This may already be implied in Gray's reluctance to publish the poem during his lifetime.) In this context, Gray's intellectually- and emotionally-driven work becomes symptomatic of the larger body of preromantic poetry. If this work is neglected, it's not because it lacks value. Rather, it's because commentators such as Wordsworth, Arnold, T. S. Eliot and F. R. Leavis have decided, for ideological as much as linguistic reasons, that 'value' lies elsewhere.

# 5

# Conclusion:
# The Future of the Pre-Romantic

This book has argued that pre-romantic poetry should be valued, both on its own terms (insofar as these can be recovered) and because it tells us important things about how literary history is formed and narrated. Returning, symbolically, to one of the arenas in which I have pursued this topic, I want to use my conclusion to argue that occasional poetry is a continuing – indeed dominant – presence in contemporary literary culture.

An example.

Chapter 3 cited Jean Baudrillard's identification of September 11, 2001 as 'the absolute event... the pure event uniting within itself all the events that have ever taken place'.[1] Despite my hostility to uncritical celebrations of the romantic sublime, I'd acknowledge that the attack on the World Trade Center baffles understanding. Chapter 3 argued, however, that culture should not abandon a commitment to analysis just because individuals experience a block to their comprehension. If anything, that commitment should be strengthened not forfeited, even if we suspect that the results will be partial or contradictory.

Despite its sublime impact, September 11 bears witness to an ongoing wish for exploration and discussion: note the vast amount of occasional writing that it has produced. Although the sheer volume of this writing indicates the scale of the 'event', the very presence of the writing suggests that the urge to understanding has not been undone. On the contrary, the countless words that have been written on the subject indicate a desire for comprehension and control that in turn marks an ongoing investment in the idea of a reflective self. (A reading self, one might say.) To be sure, that self is fragmented and contingent – but it would be, even if 9/11 had not occurred.

Most of the occasional writing generated by September 11 is, of course, journalistic. But look, too, at the myriad websites in which the day and its aftermath are memorialized through poetry. Mourners commemorate friends and relations, while those who saw the event in person or on television try to record their impressions; each anniversary becomes a prompt for further writing. The 'shock and awe' of the second Gulf War has also yielded occasional poetry. In January 2003, the Poet Laureate of Great Britain, Andrew Motion, used his official position to publish a poem ('Causa Belli') that questioned US/ British motives for intervening in Iraq. Two anthologies, 'Poets Against the War' and '100 Poets Against the War', were also published in early 2003; contributors included Adrienne Rich, W. S. Merwin, Marilyn Hacker and Minnie Bruce Pratt. A US website attached to the 'Poets Against the War' project has archived over 20,000 poetic submissions from professional and non-professional writers. In response, Charles Weatherford established a website entitled 'Poets *for* the War'; intriguingly, this site has since broadened its remit to call for a return to traditional verse forms.

Whatever the style or ideological slant of the poetry in question, it's clear that world events and global news networks have stimulated an already powerful impulse towards occasional writing. Commentators may decry the provenance of this work – it's often said that more people write poetry than read it – but its existence reveals a continuity between mid eighteenth- and early twenty-first-century poetic practice. For Wordsworth, the poet is 'a man speaking to men' – but not any man. Instead, he is 'endued with more lively sensibility, more enthusiasm, more tenderness' and 'has a greater knowledge of human nature, and a more comprehensive soul, than are supposed to be common among mankind'. How many of us will meet that challenge? Not many, especially since Wordsworth's poet must also have 'a greater readiness and power in expressing what he thinks and feels'.[2] Although Wordsworth emphasizes the language of everyday speech, the occasional poets whom he displaces embody the more democratic message that poetry can be written by servants and patrons, gentlemen and labourers, maids and professors. Moreover, these heterogeneous people

105

write about furniture, wars, desire, gin, friendship and bodily functions. Their work may have a dubious position within canons of English Literature but that in itself is a reminder that students of culture ought to look beyond the official organs through which contemporary writing is disseminated. Should they do so, they will find bodies of writing that in varying ways spring from, and address, life in the west's globalized economies.

The poets who have written for or against the war in Iraq are not, in any real sense, pre-romantic. But by indicating the persistence of occasional writing, they underline my argument that mid and late eighteenth-century poetry is not a valueless cul-de-sac. On the contrary, attention to the forms and structures of eighteenth-century poetic production may tell us more than we expect about the social and economic conditions through which twenty-first century writing circulates.

# Notes

## CHAPTER 1: PRE-ROMANTICISM AND LITERARY HISTORY

1. Marshall Brown, *Preromanticism* (Stanford: Stanford University Press, 1991), 3. Subsequent references will be to 'Brown' followed by the page number.
2. See W. Jackson Bate, *The Burden of the Past and the English Poet* (London: Chatto and Windus, 1971).
3. Brown, 2.
4. T. S. Eliot, 'Introduction' to Samuel Johnson's 'London' and 'The Vanity of Human Wishes', extracted in Eliot's *Selected Prose*, edited by John Hayward (Penguin, 1953), 157.
5. Brown, 9. F. R. Leavis is also significant: his unsympathetic account of eighteenth-century poetry refers approvingly to Eliot's essay on the Augustans. Helping to ratify the twentieth-century dismissal of Cowper *et al*, Leavis notes that this is 'a period in which something has gone wrong'. See *Revaluation: Tradition and Development in English Poetry* (London: Chatto, 1936), 101.
6. Jerome McGann, 'The Third World of Criticism' in Marjorie Levinson *et al*, *Rethinking Historicism: Critical Readings in Romantic History* (Oxford: Blackwell, 1989), 87.
7. Anne McClintock, 'The Angel of Progress: Pitfalls of the Term "Post-colonialism"' in *Social Text*, 31/32, Spring 1992, 1–15.
8. Kwame Anthony Appiah, 'Is the post- in postmodernism the post- in postcolonial?' in *Critical Inquiry*, 17, Winter 1991, 336–57.
9. Alan Sinfield, *Gay and After* (London: Serpent's Tail, 1998).
10. Patricia Duncker, 'Post-Gender: Jurassic Feminism meets Queer Politics' in Martin McQuillan *et al*, *Post-Theory: New Directions in Criticism* (Edinburgh: Edinburgh UP, 1999). Subsequent references to this collection will be given as 'McQuillan' followed by the page number.
11. Jonathan Dollimore, *Sexual Dissidence: Augustine to Wilde, Freud to Foucault* (Oxford: Clarendon Press, 1991), 72–3.

12. See Robert Young, 'Poststructuralism: The End of Theory' in *Oxford Literary Review* 5 (1982), 3–15 and 'Poststructuralism: The Improper Name' in Young's *Torn Halves: Political Conflict in Literary and Cultural Theory* (Manchester: Manchester University Press, 1996).
13. Nicholas Royle, 'Déjà Vu' in McQuillan.
14. Francis Fukuyama, 'The End of History?' in *The National Interest*, Summer 1989.
15. See Young, *Torn Halves*, 70.
16. McQuillan, 4.
17. Charlotte Brontë, *Shirley* (1849), edited by Herbert Rosengarten and Margaret Smith (Oxford: Clarendon Press, 1979), 253.
18. Donald Davie, *Purity of Diction in English Verse* (London: Chatto, 1952), 57.
19. Brown, 3.
20. Sylvia Plath, 'Context' in *Johnny Panic and the Bible of Dreams* (London: Faber, 1977), 93.
21. Jacqueline Rose uses 'textual entities' to describe the combinations of literary output and cultural fantasy that cohere around Sylvia Plath and Ted Hughes: see *The Haunting of Sylvia Plath* (London: Virago, 1991).
22. Virginia Woolf, *To The Lighthouse* (London: Grafton, 1977), 155.
23. Elizabeth Bishop, 'Efforts of Affection: A Memoir of Marianne Moore' in Bishop's *The Collected Prose* (New York: Noonday, 1984), 130.
24. See Gillian Beer, *Arguing with the Past* (London: Routledge, 1989), 3.
25. See Joseph M. Levine, *The Battle of the Books: History and Literature in the Augustan Age* (Ithaca: Cornell University Press, 1991).
26. For more on eighteenth-century Shakespearean scholarship and the emergence of literary history, see Margreta de Grazia, *Shakespeare Verbatim: The Reproduction of Authenticity and the 1790 Apparatus* (Oxford: Clarendon Press, 1991).
27. See Marilyn Butler, 'Repossessing the Past' in Marjorie Levinson *et al*, *Rethinking Historicism: Critical Readings in Romantic History* (Oxford: Blackwell, 1989), 67–8. Nicholas Royle, 'Déjà Vu' in McQuillan.

## CHAPTER 2: POETRY AND PATRONAGE

1. The *St James's Chronicle*, 11–14 June, 1791; quoted in *PWC* ii, 289–90.
2. Montagu wrote that putting her name to a 'bond or Mortgage wd appear to me a masculine action...no real harm, but merely an indecorum'; see Reginald Blunt, editor, *Mrs Montagu, 'Queen of the Blues': Her Letters and Friendships from 1762 to 1800*, 2 vols (London, 1923), ii, 18. Subsequent references will be to 'Blunt' followed by the

volume and page numbers. In the 1780s, eighty five per cent of British families would have earned less than fifty pounds a year.

3. For more on this painting, and other representations of the bluestockings, see Sylvia Harcstark Myers, *The Bluestocking Circle: Women, Friendship and the Life of the Mind in Eighteenth-Century England* (Oxford: Clarendon Press, 1990), Chapter 11. Subsequent references will be to 'Myers' followed by the page number. Also see, Elizabeth Eger, 'Representing Culture: *The Nine Living Muses of Great Britain* (1779)' in Eger *et al, Women, Writing and the Public Sphere, 1700–1830* (Cambridge: Cambridge University Press, 2001).

4. See Cowper's memoir 'Adelphi' in *LWC* i, 3–61.

5. This overview of Cowper's finances is indebted to James King, *William Cowper: A Biography* (Durham NC: Duke University Press, 1986), 59. Subsequent references will be to 'King' followed by the page number.

6. Compare Thomas Gray telling Horace Walpole to receive his latest letter 'as you would a Michaelmas Goose from a Tenant [...] I send it, not that I believe you have a taste for an awkward fat creature, but because I have no better way of showing my good-will' (*CTG* i, 49).

7. Virginia Woolf, 'The Plumage Bill' (1920) in *The Essays of Virginia Woolf*, vol. iii, edited by Andrew McNeillie (London: Hogarth, 1988), 242. Woolf's main point is that men, not women, ran the feather trade; but her distaste is clear in either case.

8. I'm using *Windsor Forest* because it is one of the best-known eighteenth-century poems about trade, not because I think that Cowper is directly echoing Pope's poem; similar parallels could be drawn with many other works, including James Thomson's *The Castle of Indolence* (1748).

9. Laura Brown, *Alexander Pope* (Oxford, 1985), 28–45.

10. For some visual instances, see Margaret W. Ferguson, 'Feathers and Flies: Aphra Behn and the seventeenth-century trade in exotica' in Margreta de Grazia, Maureen Quilligan and Peter Stallybrass, eds., *Subject and Object in Renaissance Culture* (Cambridge: Cambridge University Press, 1996).

11. See Marcia Pointon, *Hanging the Head: Portraiture and Social Formation in Eighteenth-Century England* (New Haven and London: Yale University Press, 1993), 154–5.

12. Blunt ii, 31.

13. The contemporary account in the *St James's Chronicle* notes that the 'the most brilliant colours, the produce of all climates' are 'artfully sewed together' to form 'beautiful festoons of flowers and other fanciful decorations' (quoted in Horace Walpole, *The Yale Edition of Horace Walpole's Correspondence*, edited by W. S. Lewis *et al*, 47 vols

(New Haven: Yale University Press, 1937–83), xi, 290–1).

14. The cost of feathers can be gauged from a detail in the feud that Harriot Hesketh conducted against Mary Unwin's ward, Hannah Wilson. One of Hesketh's triumphs involved depriving the 'little extravagant bitch' (as another member of the circle put it) of 'a plume of white feathers which were to come to 5 guineas' (King, 262; emphasis in original). Other sources confirm that single plumes would sell, in the middle of the century, for a guinea apiece: for this and other details about the use of feathers in eighteenth-century fashion, see Aileen Ribeiro, *Dress in Eighteenth-Century Europe, 1715–1789* (New Haven and London: Yale University Press, 2002), 91, 109, 149, 170, 236, 266, 270.

15. See Arthur Charles Fox-Davies, *A Complete Guide to Heraldry* (London: Nelson, 1909), 233–52.

16. Although Montagu was a gentlewoman rather than an aristocrat, she mixed with the nobility from an early age. Her mother was an heiress with property in Cambridgeshire and Kent, while her father had land in Yorkshire. With three older brothers (and several younger ones), Montagu could not have hoped to inherit much from her parents; however her marriage more than made up for the shortfall. See Myers, 21–30.

17. Blunt, ii, 136. For more on Montagu's work as patron and magnate, see Betty Rizzo, *Companions Without Vows: Relationships Among Eighteenth-Century British Women* (Athens GA and London: University of Georgia Press, 1994).

18. Blunt ii, 207.

19. Elsewhere Cowper refers to the 'swarthy Brethren of the Mine' who work where 'Humber pours his rich Commercial Stream' (*PWC* i, 215–6).

20. For more on Betty Tull's labours, see Blunt, ii, 112, 201, 202, 228.

21. King, 223. Horace Walpole ignored all the approaches but Thurlow was eventually persuaded by one of Cowper's relatives, the Clerk Assistant to the House of Lords. The ups and downs of the pursuit are summarized in King, 197–225.

22. In Greek legend, Arion was carried to safety by a dolphin who heard him sing before he was thrown overboard by unscrupulous sailors.

23. Cowper's version of Thurlow (who was notoriously boorish) would not have been recognized by many of their contemporaries. See *PWC* i, 544.

24. See, for example, *LWC* i, 488; *LWC* ii, 293.

25. Clare Brant points out that eighteenth-century letters were far from 'private' – not only were they often read aloud, they were also the primary form through which social and political business was

conducted. See Clare Brant, *Eighteenth-Century Letters and British Culture* (Basingstoke: Palgrave, 2006).

26. Cowper had 498; Pope had 574 for his *Iliad* and 654 for his *Odyssey*. See *LWC* iii, 504.

27. For an interesting analysis of the relationship between primitivism and education, see Chapter 4 of Richard Greene's *Mary Leapor: A Study in Eighteenth-Century Women's Poetry* (Oxford: Clarendon Press, 1993). For contrasting readings of Yearsley and working-class women's poetry, see Donna Landry, *The Muses of Resistance: Laboring-Class Women's Poetry in Britain, 1739–1796* (Cambridge: Cambridge University Press, 1990) and Mary Waldron, *Lactilla, the Milkwoman of Clifton* (Georgia: University of Georgia Press, 1996).

28. Blunt ii, 185.


## CHAPTER 3: THE OCCASIONS OF POETRY

1. Thom Gunn, 'Ben Jonson' in *The Occasions of Poetry* (San Francisco: North Point Press, 1985), 106. Subsequent references will be given as 'Gunn' followed by the page number.

2. Although I don't draw on them directly, my analysis here and elsewhere in this chapter is broadly in line with the approaches taken in Jerome McGann's *The Romantic Ideology* (Chicago: Chicago University Press, 1983) and Clifford Siskin's *The Historicity of Romantic Discourse* (Oxford: Oxford Uuniversity Press, 1988).

3. Gunn, 106.

4. John Dolan, *Poetic Occasion from Milton to Wordsworth* (Basingstoke: Macmillan, 2000), 2, 6. Subsequent references will be to 'Dolan' followed by the page number. Although I would question Dolan's emphasis on funereal verse over kinds of occasion (e.g. births, marriages and engagements) I certainly support his larger thought that notions of the poetic 'occasion' are redefined and expanded over the course of the eighteenth century.

5. It's also dangerous to assume that patronage poems are inevitably elitist. By definition, patrons hold access to political or financial power; poems addressed to them are likely to uphold certain hierarchies. However the position from which the poet writes is not, in itself, a privileged one. Many disadvantaged writers maintained decidedly prickly relations with their backers: James Woodhouse's verse novel *The Life and Lucubrations of Crispinus Scriblerus* (written between 1795 and 1800, published 1896) is less than positive about Elizabeth Montagu, who employed him as a bailiff. (He was, by trade, a cobbler.)

6. Samuel Johnson, *Lives of the English Poets*, edited by George Birkbeck

Hill, 3 vols (Hildesheim: Olms, 1968), iii, 434.

7. Vincent Newey, *Cowper's Poetry: A Critical Study and Reassessment* (Liverpool: Liverpool University Press, 1982), 232. Subsequent references will be given as 'Newey' followed by the page number.

8. Newey 235.

9. Newey 224 and 227.

10. Newey 228; emphasis in original.

11. Conrad Brunström, *William Cowper: Religion, Satire, Religion* (Lewisburg: Bucknell University Press, 2004), 172–3. Subsequent references will be given as 'Brunström' followed by the page number.

12. Brunström 15.

13. Alan Sinfield, *Shakespeare, Authority, Sexuality: Unfinished Business in Cultural Materialism* (London and New York: Routledge, 2006), 4; emphasis in the original.

14. W. K. Wimsatt, *The Verbal Icon: Studies in the Meaning of Poetry* (Lexington: Kentucky University Press, 1954), 231; emphasis in the original. Subsequent references will be to 'Wimsatt' followed by the page number.

15. Cleanth Brooks, *The Well Wrought Urn: Studies in the Structure of Poetry* (London: Dobson, 1949), ii.

16. For example, see *Language Machines: Technologies of Literary and Cultural Production*, edited by Jeffrey Masten *et al* (London and New York: Routledge, 1997) and Roger Chartier's *Forms and Meanings: Texts, Performances and Audiences from Codex to Computer* (Philadelphia: University of Pennsylvania Press, 1995).

17. For a stimulating reading of the Chapman sonnet, see Daniel P. Watkins, *Keats's Poetry and the Politics of the Imagination* (London and Toronto: Associated University Presses, 1989), 26–31. On Keats's general relationship to materiality, Marjorie Levinson argues that 'for Keats, the initiative is always and fundamentally on the side of the object world'; see Levinson's *Keats's Life of Allegory: The Origins of a Style* (Oxford, 1988), 242.

18. Wimsatt 100.

19. Poems cannot be 'open' or 'closed' in any literal sense: these terms are simply ways of exploring the impact that certain stylistic effects have upon the reader.

20. Jean-François Lyotard, 'The Sublime and the Avant-Garde' (1984) in *The Lyotard Reader*, edited by Andrew Benjamin (Oxford: Blackwell, 1989), 199–200; my emphasis. Subsequent references will be to 'Lyotard' followed by the page number.

21. Jean-François Lyotard, 'Answering the Question: What is Postmodernism?' collected in *The Postmodern Condition: A Report on Knowledge* (Manchester: Manchester University Press, 1986), 71–82.

22. Lyotard 203–4.

23. Immanuel Kant, *Critique of Judgement*, translated by Werner S. Pluhar (Indianapolis: Hackett, 1987), 98; emphasis in original.
24. I am greatly endebted to Sophie Thomas's *Romanticism and Visuality: Fragments, History, Spectacle* (New York: Routledge, 2008), which deals extensively with literary and visual fragmentation. Also see Thomas McFarland's *Romanticism and the Forms of Ruin: Wordsworth, Coleridge, and Modalities of Fragmentation* (Princeton, 1981), Marjorie Levinson's *The Romantic Fragment Poem: A Critique of a Form* (Chapel Hill and London, 1986), Anne Janowitz's *England's Ruins: Poetic Purpose and the National Landscape* (Oxford, 1990) and Elizabeth Wanning Harries's *The Unfinished Manner: Essays on the Fragment in the Later Eighteenth Century* (Charlottesville and London, 1994).
25. William Wordsworth, *The Oxford Authors*, edited by Stephen Gill (Oxford: Oxford University Press, 1984), 262; subsequent references will be to 'Wordsworth' followed by the page number. Wordsworth's phrase comes from 'Resolution and Independence' (written 1802, published 1807). Wordsworth also calls Chatterton a 'Boy' in his 'Essay, Supplementary to the Preface' (1815): see Wordsworth, 656.
26. Keats's poem on the Elgin marbles illustrates this paradox. Although Keats stresses the gap between 'Grecian grandeur' and 'the rude / Wasting of old Time', he expresses this thought via an impeccably organized sonnet: his chosen form makes no attempt to ape the erosion it describes. See John Keats, *The Complete Poems*, edited by John Barnard, revised third edition (Harmondsworth: Penguin, 2003), 100; subsequent references will be to 'Keats' followed by the page number. The same could be said of several of Keats's other sonnets, as well as of Shelley's 'Ozymandias'.
27. Gunn 106.
28. J. D. McClatchy, 'Feces' in *Hazmat* (New York: Knopf, 2002), 27.
29. 'The Study of Poetry' (1880) in Matthew Arnold, *English Literature and Irish Politics*, edited by R. H. Super (Ann Arbor: University of Michigan Press, 1973), 180–1. Subsequent references will be given as 'Arnold' followed by the page number.
30. S. T. Coleridge, *Biographia Literaria*, edited by Nigel Leask (London: Everyman, 1997), 11; emphasis in original.
31. Wordsworth, 650.
32. See *Genesis*, 1–2 for Creation, and Genesis 11 for the destruction of the Tower of Babel.
33. Sylvia Plath, *The Bell Jar* (London: Faber, 1986), 131.
34. Sylvia Plath, *The Journals of Sylvia Plath 1950–1962*, edited by Karen V. Kukil (London: Faber, 2000), 360.
35. Sylvia Plath, *Collected Poems* (London: Faber, 1981), 204.
36. Lyotard 197.

37. Lyotard 199; emphasis in the original.
38. Edmund Burke, *A Philosophical Enquiry into the Origin of our Ideas of the Sublime and the Beautiful*, edited by Adam Phillips (Oxford: Oxford University Press, 1990), 53.
39. Lyotard 204–5; my emphasis.
40. Jean Baudrillard, *The Spirit of Terrorism* (London and New York: Verso, 2003), 4. Subsequent references will be given as 'Baudrillard' followed by the page number.
41. Lyotard 204–5.
42. Baudrillard 12–13. *Beyond Good and Evil* (1886) is one of Nietzsche's best-known books.
43. Baudrillard 9.
44. John Keats, *The Letters of John Keats*, selected and edited by Robert Gittings, revised edition (Oxford, 1992), 157–8.
45. 'John Keats' (1880) in Arnold, 206.
46. Paul H. Fry, *A Defense of Poetry: Reflections on the Occasion of Writing* (Stanford: Stanford University Press, 1995), 127.
47. 'Wordsworth' (1879) in Arnold, 48 and 43; emphasis in the original.
48. Although I don't refer to it directly, my approach here is influenced by Alan Sinfield's *Cultural Politics – Queer Reading* (London: Routledge, 1994).
49. Roger Lonsdale, 'Introduction' to *Eighteenth-Century Women Poets: An Oxford Anthology* (Oxford: Oxford University Press, 1989), pp. xl–xli.
50. In particular, see William Duff, *An Essay on Original Genius* (1767).
51. Although they take an unconventional form, Cowper's emotional relations are directed almost entirely toward women; I'm therefore unpersuaded by Andrew Elfenbein's seductive attempt to claim Cowper for homosexuality. See Elfenbein, *Romantic Genius: The Prehistory of a Homosexual Role* (New York: Columbia University Press, 1999), 63–89
52. Wordsworth, 601–2.

## CHAPTER 4: HOMOEROTICISM AND THE PASTORAL

1. Although Lee's adaptation was widely described as a gay cowboy movie, its lead characters herd sheep, not cows.
2. For an account of the idealizing tendencies of pastoral criticism, see Chapter 2 of Alan Sinfield, *Shakespeare, Authority, Sexuality: Unfinished Business in Cultural Materialism* (London and New York, 2006).
3. See Raymond Williams, *The Country and the City* (London: Chatto, 1973), James Turner, *Politics of Landscape* (Oxford: Blackwell, 1979),

John Barrell, *English Literature in History 1730–1780: An Equal, Wide Survey* (London: Hutchinson, 1983), and Roger Sales, *English Literature in History 1780–1830: Pastoral and Politics* (London: Hutchinson, 1983).

4. For a summary of the varied, and not always flattering, ways in which Augustus was used in the eighteenth century, see the final chapter of James Sambrook's *The Eighteenth Century: The Intellectual and Cultural Context of English Literature, 1700–1789*, second edition (Harlow, 1993).

5. He wrote them in 1704 although they were first published in 1707.

6. For instance, Virgil's first and ninth *Eclogues*.

7. William Kenrick, *Love in the Suds* (London: printed for J. Wheble, 1772), 8–9. Attic means Greek. Petronius was a Roman satirist associated with Nero's dissolute court.

8. I discuss this poem, Theocritus's fifth *Idyll*, below.

9. See *Theocritus*, edited with a commentary and translation by A. S. F. Gow, 2 vols (Cambridge University Press, 1950), i, 43 and 49.

10. Richard Barnfield, *The Complete Poems*, edited by George Klawitter (London and Toronto: Associated University Presses, 1990), 79–80.

11. *The Yale Edition of the Shorter Poems of Edmund Spenser*, edited by William A. Oram *et al* (New Haven and London: Yale University Press, 1989), 33–4. See Jonathan Goldberg, 'Colin to Hobbinol: Spenser's Familiar Letters', in *Displacing Homophobia: Gay Male Perspectives in Literature and Culture*, edited by Ronald R. Butters *et al* (Durham and London: Duke University Press, 1989), 107–126 for a reading of the Colin/Hobbinol friendship and its relation to E. K.'s glosses. Alcibiades features in several of Plato's *Dialogues*; Lucian was a second-century satirist; the Italian poet Unico Aretino was born in 1465 but E. K. presumably means another Italian writer, Pietro Aretino, who was born in 1492 and had a reputation as a pornographer; Perionius was a sixteenth-century humanist who condemned physical expressions of male-male love.

12. Although women's access to classical learning was highly restricted, middle-class blue-stocking writers such as Elizabeth Montagu and the poet and translator Elizabeth Carter often traded Greek and Roman allusions. More daringly, Anne Lister judged potential lovers by their responsiveness to well-chosen classical texts.

13. Ironically the poem in question – number twelve from Horace's fourth book of *Odes* – may refer to a different Virgil, not to the poet. Be that as it may, West, in common with earlier commentators, believed that Horace was referring to the Virgil who wrote the *Eclogues*.

14. See *Numbers* 13 and *Samson Agonistes* ll. 148 and 528.

15. Although West's reference can't be traced to a specific text, he

seems to have a fairytale such as Perrault's in mind. The Grimm Brothers' 'Hansel and Gretel' (1812) is a variation on 'Little Thumb'.

16. Horace Walpole, *The Yale Edition of Horace Walpole's Correspondence*, edited by W.S. Lewis *et al*, 47 vols (New Haven: Yale University Press, 1937–83), xxviii, 125.

17. John Sitter, *Literary Loneliness in Mid-Eighteenth-Century England* (Ithaca and London: Cornell University Press, 1982), 85–6.

18. Jean Hagstrum, *Eros and Vision: The Restoration to Romanticism* (Evanston: Northwestern University Press, 1989), 153. Subsequent references will be to 'Hagstrum' followed by the page number.

19. See Loftus Jestin, *The Answer to the Lyre: Richard Bentley's Illustrations for Thomas Gray's Poems* (Philadelphia: University of Pennsylvania Press, 1990).

20. See Pierre Macherey, *A Theory of Literary Production*, translated by Geoffrey Wall (London: Routledge, 1978), 85–95.

21. 'The poem ends...in the anxiety of sexual fulfilment and "trembling" desire...'The bosom of his Father"...sexualizes the prospect of heavenly life', George Haggerty, '"The Voice of Nature" in Gray's "Elegy"' in *Homosexuality in Renaissance and Enlightenment England*, edited by Claude Summers (New York: Harrignton Park Press, 1992), 212. Haggerty develops his account of Gray in *Men in Love: Masculinity and Sexuality in the Eighteenth Century* (New York: Columbia University Press, 1999).

22. 'Thomas Gray' (1880) in Matthew Arnold, *English Literature and Irish Politics*, edited by R.H. Super (Ann Arbor: University of Michigan Press, 1973), 189; the emphasis is Arnold's.

23 *GCG* 329, '(Quod tibi crescit opus)'.

24. *GCG* 332, 'Cum Tu opere in medio, spes tanti et causa laboris / Linquis, et aeternam fati te condis in umbram!'.

25. *GCG* 332, 'quod possum, iuxta lugere sepulcrum / Dum iuvat, et mutae vana haec iactare favillae'.

26. See, for example, Milton's 'On Shakespeare' (1632) and Robert Herrick's 'His Poetry His Pillar' (1648).

27. See *GCG* 200, note 144.

## CHAPTER 5: CONCLUSION: THE FUTURE OF THE PRE-ROMANTIC

1. Jean Baudrillard, *The Spirit of Terrorism* (London and New York: Verso, 2003), 4.

2. William Wordsworth, *The Oxford Authors*, edited by Stephen Gill (Oxford: Oxford University Press, 1984), 603–4.

# Select Bibliography

Arnold, Matthew, *English Literature and Irish Politics*, edited by R. H. Super (Ann Arbor: University of Michigan Press, 1973). Provides an invaluable insight into the Victorian reception of eighteenth-century and Romantic poetry.

Barrell, John, *English Literature in History 1730–1780: An Equal, Wide Survey* (London: Hutchinson, 1983). Cultural materialist analysis of the eighteenth-century pastoral.

Bate, W. Jackson, *The Burden of the Past and the English Poet* (London: Chatto and Windus, 1971). Influential enquiry into questions of literary influence.

Beer, Gillian, *Arguing with the Past* (London: Routledge, 1989). A useful riposte to linear versions of literary history.

Brant, Clare, *Eighteenth-Century Letters and British Culture* (Basingstoke: Palgrave, 2006). Fascinating and enormously detailed; a definitive account of the subject.

Brown, Laura, *Alexander Pope* (Oxford, 1985). Shows what can be done when critical theory is brought to bear on eighteenth-century poetry.

Brown, Marshall, *Preromanticism* (Stanford: Stanford University Press, 1991). Deals with pre-romantic prose as well as poetry; an impressive achievement, though sometimes questionable in its assumptions.

Brunström, Conrad, *William Cowper: Religion, Satire, Religion* (Lewisburg: Bucknell University Press, 2004).

Coleridge, S. T., *Biographia Literaria*, edited by Nigel Leask (London: Everyman, 1997). One of the monuments of English criticism – often questions or qualifies Wordsworth's literary judgements.

Cowper, William, *The Letters and Prose Writings of William Cowper*, edited by James King and Charles Ryskamp, 5 vols (Oxford: Clarendon Press, 1979–1986). Cowper's enormously entertaining letters are brimming with fascinating social and literary observations.

——, *The Poems of William Cowper*, edited by John H. Baird and Charles Ryskamp, 3 vols (Oxford: Clarendon Press, 1980–1995).

117

Curran, Stuart, *Poetic Form and British Romanticism* (Oxford: Oxford University Press, 1986).

Davie, Donald, *Purity of Diction in English Verse* (London: Chatto, 1952). Classic analysis of the technical aspects of English poetry.

De Man, Paul, *Blindness and Insight: ssays in the rhetoric of contemporary criticism* (Oxford: Oxford University Press, 1971).

Dolan, John, *Poetic Occasion from Milton to Wordsworth* (Basingstoke: Macmillan, 2000). A serious account of a much neglected topic.

Eger, Elizabeth, *et al*, *Women, Writing and the Public Sphere, 1700-1830* (Cambridge: Cambridge University Press, 2001).

Elfenbein, Andrew, *Romantic Genius: The Prehistory of a Homosexual Role* (New York: Columbia University Press, 1999). Original and engaging, if sometimes debatable in its conclusions.

Fry, Paul H., *A Defense of Poetry: Reflections on the Occasion of Writing* (Stanford: Stanford University Press, 1995).

Gleckner, Robert F., *Gray Agonistes: Thomas Gray and masculine friendship* (Baltimore: Johns Hopkins University Press, 1997).

Gray, Thomas, *Correspondence of Thomas Gray*, edited by Paget Toynbee and Leonard Whibley, with corrections and additions by H.W. Starr, 3 vols (Oxford: Clarendon Press, 1971). Gray's poems are transformed when read via the letters in which they first appeared.

——, *et al*, *The Poems of Thomas Gray, William Collins and Oliver Goldsmith*, edited by Roger Lonsdale (London and New York: Longman, 1969).

Greene, Richard, *Mary Leapor: A Study in Eighteenth-Century Women's Poetry* (Oxford: Clarendon Press, 1993).

Haggerty, George, *Men in Love: Masculinity and Sexuality in the Eighteenth Century* (New York: Columbia University Press, 1999). An important contribution to a growing field.

Hagstrum, Jean, *Eros and Vision: The Restoration to Romanticism* (Evanston: Northwestern University Press, 1989). One of the first collections to think about gender and sexuality in relation to eighteenth-century writing.

Hutchings, W. B., and Ruddick, William, eds, *Thomas Gray: Contemporary Essays* (Liverpool: Liverpool University Press, 1993).

Janowitz, Anne, *England's Ruins: Poetic Purpose and the National Landscape* (Oxford, 1990).

Jestin, Loftus, *The Answer to the Lyre: Richard Bentley's Illustrations for Thomas Gray's Poems* (Philadelphia: University of Pennsylvania Press, 1990). A facsimile edition of the first volume of Gray's poetry. Jestin's commentary reasserts the importance of Bentley's collaboration with Gray; the resulting volume is both beautiful and illuminating.

Johnson, Samuel, *Lives of the English Poets*, edited by George Birkbeck

Hill, 3 vols (Hildesheim: Olms, 1968). Querulous and idiosyncratic, but always readable; an enormously important guide to the emerging canon of English poetry.

Kaul, Suvir, *Thomas Gray and Literary Authority: ideology and poetics in eighteenth-century England* (Oxford: Oxford University Press, 1992).

Keats, John, *The Complete Poems*, edited by John Barnard, revised third edition (Harmondsworth: Penguin, 2003).

————, *The Letters of John Keats*, selected and edited by Robert Gittings, revised edition (Oxford, 1992). As well as containing some of the most enjoyable letters in the language, Keats's correspondence is packed with penetrating, impressionistic comments on his contemporaries and predecessors.

King, James, *William Cowper: A Biography* (Durham NC: Duke University Press, 1986).

Labbe, Jacqueline, *Charlotte Smith: Romanticism, poetry and the culture of gender* (Manchester: Manchester University Press, 2003).

Landry, Donna, *The Muses of Resistance: Laboring-Class Women's Poetry in Britain, 1739-1796* (Cambridge: Cambridge University Press, 1990).

Leavis, F.R., *Revaluation: Tradition and Development in English Poetry* (London: Chatto, 1936). Includes some tersely negative comments on eighteenth-century poetry.

Levinson, Marjorie, *et al*, *Rethinking Historicism: Critical Readings in Romantic History* (Oxford: Blackwell, 1989). Contains useful essays on literary historical issues by four major critics.

————, *Keats's Life of Allegory: The Origins of a Style* (Oxford, 1988).

————, *The Romantic Fragment Poem: A Critique of a Form* (Chapel Hill and London, 1986).

Lonsdale, Roger, *Eighteenth-Century Women Poets: An Oxford Anthology* (Oxford: Oxford University Press, 1989). Lonsdale's two anthologies of eighteenth-century poetry re-map the field to stunning effect.

————, *The New Oxford Book of Eighteenth-Century Verse* (Oxford: Oxford University Press, 1984).

Lyotard, Jean-François, *The Lyotard Reader*, edited by Andrew Benjamin (Oxford: Blackwell, 1989).

Macherey, Pierre, *A Theory of Literary Production*, translated by Geoffrey Wall (London: Routledge, 1978). Although it focuses on prose, Macherey's work can be used to think about the gaps and silences in pre-romantic poetry.

McGann, Jerome, *The Romantic Ideology* (Chicago: Chicago Univerity Press, 1983).

McGann, Roger, *The Poetics of Sensibility: A Revolution in Literary Style* (Oxford: Oxford University Press, 1996). An eloquent reappraisal of late-eighteenth-century poetry; particularly strong on neglected female writers.

Milton, John, *The Major Works*, edited by Stephen Orgel and Jonathan Goldberg (Oxford: World's Classics, 2008). It is hard to overestimate Milton's influence on eighteenth-century poetry.

Montagu, Elizabeth, *Mrs Montagu, 'Queen of the Blues': Her Letters and Friendships from 1762 to 1800*, edited by Reginald Blunt, 2 vols (London: 1923).

Myers, Sylvia Harcstark, *The Bluestocking Circle: Women, Friendship and the Life of the Mind in Eighteenth-Century England* (Oxford: Clarendon Press, 1990).

Newey, Vincent, *Centring the Self: subjectivity, society and reading from Thomas Gray to Thomas Hardy* (Aldershot: Scolar Press, 1995).

Newey, Vincent, *Cowper's Poetry: A Critical Study and Reassessment* (Liverpool: Liverpool University Press, 1982).

Pointon, Marcia, *Hanging the Head: Portraiture and Social Formation in Eighteenth-Century England* (New Haven and London: Yale University Press, 1993). Although this is primarily a work of art history, Pointon's investigations of selfhood illuminate the poetical self-presentations of writers such as Cowper and Gray.

Pope, Alexander, *The Poems of Alexander Pope: A One-Volume Edition of the Twickenham Text with Selected Annotations*, edited by John Butt (Bungay: Methuen, 1963).

Rizzo, Betty, *Companions Without Vows: Relationships Among Eighteenth-Century British Women* (Athens GA and London: University of Georgia Press, 1994). Has a useful chapter on Elizabeth Montagu.

Rothstein, Eric, *Restoration and Eighteenth-Century Poetry, 1660–1780* (London: Routledge and Kegan Paul, 1981). Provides a helpful guide to the forms and structures of eighteenth-century poetry; includes a useful chronology.

Sales, Roger, *English Literature in History 1780–1830: Pastoral and Politics* (London: Hutchinson, 1983). Polemical, Marxist-influenced analysis of the topic.

Sambrook, James, *The Eighteenth Century: The Intellectual and Cultural Context of English Literature, 1700–1789*, second edition (Harlow, 1993). Very useful overview of the period; especially helpful on philosophy and literary fashion.

Sinfield, Alan, *Cultural Politics – Queer Reading* (London: Routledge, 1994). Although Sinfield's book deals primarily with twentieth-century materials, his ways of thinking about reading and sexuality are valuable in relation to other historical periods.

———, *Shakespeare, Authority, Sexuality: Unfinished Business in Cultural Materialism* (London and New York: Routledge, 2006). Includes an invigorating chapter on pastoral writing.

Siskin, Clifford, *The Historicity of Romantic Discourse* (Oxford: Oxford University Press, 1988). A polemical reappraisal of Romanticism and its critical reception/construction.

Sitter, John, *Literary Loneliness in Mid-Eighteenth-Century England* (Ithaca and London: Cornell University Press, 1982). A suggestive reading of literary solitude: especially helpful for thinking about Thomas Gray.

Spenser, Edmund, *The Yale Edition of the Shorter Poems of Edmund Spenser*, edited by Oram, William A., *et al* (New Haven and London: Yale University Press, 1989). With Milton, Spenser is one of the major influences on eighteenth-century poetry.

Summers, Claude, editor, *Homosexuality in Renaissance and Enlightenment England*, (New York: Harrington Park Press, 1992).

Thomas, Sophie, *Romanticism and Visuality: Fragments, History, Spectacle* (New York: Routledge, 2008). A fascinating and exemplary analysis of Romantic period discourse.

Turner, James, *Politics of Landscape* (Oxford: Blackwell, 1979).

Waldron, Mary, *Lactilla, the Milkwoman of Clifton* (Georgia: University of Georgia Press, 1996).

Walpole, Horace, *The Yale Edition of Horace Walpole's Correspondence*, edited by W.S. Lewis *et al*, 47 vols (New Haven: Yale University Press, 1937–83). The whole of eighteenth-century literary life lies within these pages.

Watkins, Daniel P., *Keats's Poetry and the Politics of the Imagination* (London and Toronto: Associated University Presses, 1989).

William Wordsworth, *The Oxford Authors*, edited by Stephen Gill (Oxford: Oxford University Press, 1984). As well as reprinting Wordsworth's major poems, this volume contains a generous selection of his critical writing.

Williams, Raymond, *The Country and the City* (London: Chatto, 1973). One of the first books to read pastoral writing through Marxism; still useful – and readable.

# Index

Lightning Source UK Ltd.
Milton Keynes UK
UKOW031523260612

195099UK00001B/14/P